This Book belongs to

_____

_____

Gift From

_____

Date _____

Whatever you do, do everything for the Glory of God.

1 Cor 10:31

My Daily Spiritual Companion

A Record of
Birthdays and Anniversaries
with a
Saint of the Day Thought
and Prayer for Every Day
of the Year

MARCI ALBORGHETTI

CATHOLIC BOOK PUBLISHING CORP.
NEW JERSEY

Nihil Obstat:
Rev. Msgr. James M. Cafone, M.A., S.T.D.
Censor Librorum

Imprimatur:
✢ Most Rev. John J. Myers, J.C.D., D.D.
Archbishop of Newark

Illustrations by: Geoffrey Butz

(T-380)

© 2008 Catholic Book Publishing Corp.
Printed in Korea
www.catholicbookpublishing.com

— BIRTHFLOWERS —

January........ Snowdrop *for Friendship*

February ...... Violet *for Modesty*

March........... Daffodil *for Affection*

April............. Daisy *for Tenacity*

May .... Lily of the Valley *for Happiness*

June .... Rose *for Devotion*

July .... Larkspur *for Open-heartedness*

August .... Poppy *for Commitment*

September .... Morning Glory *for Devotion*

October......... Marigold *for Excellence*

November ..... Chrysanthemum *for Compassion*

December ..... Holly *for Success*

— BIRTHSTONES —

January .... Garnet *for Constancy*

February ...... Amethyst *for Sincerity*

March .... Aquamarine *for Respect*

April .... Diamond *for Innocence*

May .... Emerald *for Happiness*

June .... Pearl *for Purity*

July .... Ruby *for Nobility*

August .... Peridot *for Love*

September .... Sapphire *for Wisdom*

October .... Opal *for Hope*

November ..... Topaz *for Fidelity*

December ..... Turquoise *for Success*

Sing to the Lord a new song, His praise in the Assembly of the Saints.

Ps 149:1

JANUARY 1st

Mary, the Mother of God

We begin the New Year with Mary, whose resolution to obey God and bear His Son made salvation possible for all of us.

Today is the Birthday of:

_____

_____

Today is the Anniversary of:

_____

_____

Prayer: *Mary, help me to make and keep those New Year's resolutions that will bring me closer to your Son and align me with His will.*

JANUARY 2nd

St. Adalhard, Abbot

Like Saint Adalhard, we should spend more energy on our spiritual treasures than material treasures.

Today is the Birthday of:

Today is the Anniversary of:

Prayer: *Beloved Jesus, You warned against trying to serve God and money; give me the strength to serve God and do Your work on earth.*

JANUARY 3rd

The Most Holy Name of Jesus

When we are concerned and disturbed by the noise of the world, we need only speak Jesus' holy name and find peace.

Today is the Birthday of:

Today is the Anniversary of:

Prayer: *Lord, teach me to call on Your name at all hours of the day and night, whenever I need help.*

JANUARY 4th

Saint Elizabeth Ann Seton

Just as Saint Elizabeth cared for her sick husband and children before founding Catholic schools, we seek to carry our worldly burdens with grace.

Today is the Birthday of:

Today is the Anniversary of:

Prayer: *Father, help me to care for my family even as I seek to do Your work in the wider world.*

JANUARY 5th

∽∾∽

Saint John Neumann, Bishop

Through our words and actions we should bring Jesus' message to everyone, especially immigrants, strangers, and the poor.

❦   ❦   ❦

Today is the Birthday of:

_____

_____

Today is the Anniversary of:

_____

_____

Prayer: *Lord, teach me to be a true evangelist, bringing Your words and works not just to those I know well, but to everyone You put in my life.*

JANUARY 6th

Saint Charles of Sezze

In the spirit of Saint Charles of Sezze, we do not let our limitations stop us in our journey toward God.

Today is the Birthday of:

Today is the Anniversary of:

Prayer: *Faithful Lord, I pray to show the kind of devotion to the Lord that is embodied in Saint Charles and January's flower the snowdrop.*

JANERY 7th

Saint Lucian of Antioch

A great intellectual, Saint Lucian reminds us that we may advance closer to God by studying scripture and the gospels.

Today is the Birthday of:

Today is the Anniversary of:

Prayer: *Dear God, open my mind to You in all that You have created, from the heavens and the earth, to the mysteries of the Bible.*

JANUARY 8th

Saint Apollinaris, Bishop

With Saint Apollinaris, we recognize the answers to prayer that ease our way on earth and bring us nearer to God.

Today is the Birthday of:

Today is the Anniversary of:

Prayer: *Father, everywhere I go there are small and large signs of Your presence for the good in my life; open my eyes to them and You.*

JANUARY 9th

St. Adrian of Canterbury, Abbot

A brilliant scholar and administrator, Saint Adrian was born in Africa, reminding us that we belong to a worldwide religion.

Today is the Birthday of:

Today is the Anniversary of:

Prayer: *Lord, help me to embrace in my thoughts, words, and actions people from every race, ethnicity, and religion who belong to You.*

JANUARY 10th

St. Peter Orseolo

We strive to be like Saint Peter Orseolo who abandoned the life of a successful government leader to give himself completely to God.

Today is the Birthday of:

Today is the Anniversary of:

Prayer: *I pray for the discernment to hear and obey God when He calls me to make changes in my life.*

JANUARY 11th

St. Paulinus, Patriarch of Aquileia

Like Paulinus, we seek to make converts not by force or disdain, but by our visible love of Jesus.

Today is the Birthday of:

Today is the Anniversary of:

Prayer: *Jesus, Lord, help me to follow Your blessed example and to show others Your face through my loving words and actions.*

JANUARY 12th

St. Margaret Bourgeoys

Like Saint Margaret Bourgeoys, the first Canadian Saint, we should teach and nurture the poor, especially poor children.

Today is the Birthday of:

Today is the Anniversary of:

Prayer: *Generous Lord Jesus, help me to give of my money and my time to children in need.*

JANUARY 13th

Bl. Yvette (Jutta) of Huy

As a young widow and mother of three, Blessed Yvette teaches us to avoid self-pity and to search for God's presence in our adversity.

Today is the Birthday of:

Today is the Anniversary of:

Prayer: *I pray for the courage and strength to overcome life's setbacks and difficulties as I find comfort, strength, and renewal in God.*

JANUARY 14th

St. Nino

Enslaved by men, but free in God, Saint Nino shows us that our worldly state is no obstacle to our relationship with God.

Today is the Birthday of:

Today is the Anniversary of:

Prayer: *Creator God, help me to remember that You made me to be Your very own child, regardless of my circumstances.*

JANARY 15th

St. Ita

We know through Saint Ita, teacher of Saints, that true faith is a simple matter of loving God and living righteously.

Today is the Birthday of:

Today is the Anniversary of:

Prayer: *Lord, remind me that to follow You I need only love and obey You and treat others kindly.*

JANUARY 16th

St. Marcellus I, Pope

Even when politics and governments make it difficult to be a Christian, like St. Marcellus, we must follow Jesus and not lose hope.

Today is the Birthday of:

Today is the Anniversary of:

Prayer: *Jesus, it is unlikely that I will ever face the persecution that You and Saint Marcellus faced, but help me to meet the challenges of my days with trust and fortitude in You.*

JANUARY 17th

St. Anthony

Through Saint Anthony, abbot and hermit, we understand that solitude is vital if we wish to meditate on and approach God.

Today is the Birthday of:

Today is the Anniversary of:

Prayer: *Father, teach me that by giving myself to You in silence and meditation and quietude, I am also giving myself the gift of Your awe-inspiring Presence.*

JANUARY 18th

Bl. Christina Ciccarelli

Like Blessed Christina, our love for Jesus should be evident for all to see in our deep humility and obedient actions.

Today is the Birthday of:

Today is the Anniversary of:

Prayer: *Jesus, let my devotion to You be so joyful that my feet hardly touch the ground, even when I suffer hardships as I do Your work.*

JANARY 19th

～～

Sts. Marius, Martha, Audifax, and Abachum, Martyrs

With this saintly family, we follow Jesus in serving the poor of the whole human family.

☙   ☙   ☙

Today is the Birthday of:

⸻⸻⸻⸻⸻⸻⸻⸻⸻

⸻⸻⸻⸻⸻⸻⸻⸻⸻

⸻⸻⸻⸻⸻⸻⸻⸻⸻

Today is the Anniversary of:

⸻⸻⸻⸻⸻⸻⸻⸻⸻

⸻⸻⸻⸻⸻⸻⸻⸻⸻

Prayer: *Father of us all, give me the courage to make do with less so that I and my family can give more to those in need.*

JANURARY 20th

St. Sebastian, Martyr

While few of us face torture and death for our faith, we pray for the many Christians who are still persecuted.

Today is the Birthday of:

Today is the Anniversary of:

Prayer: *Father, make me strong enough to speak and act in Your name and on behalf of Your people even in the face of danger.*

JANUARY 21st

St. Agnes, Martyr

Saint Agnes shows that answering the Lord's call is not easy, but by choosing Him we receive our heart's desire.

Today is the Birthday of:

Today is the Anniversary of:

Prayer: *Beloved Lord, help me to follow my vocation, listening to and following You in all that I do and become in my life.*

JANUARY 22nd

Bl. Laura Vicuna

Blessed Laura's innocence, in spite of being abused, teaches us the wisdom of child-like faith.

Today is the Birthday of:

Today is the Anniversary of:

Prayer: *Jesus, help me to follow Blessed Laura's example and make my faith simple, complete, perfect.*

JANUARY 23rd

St. Ildefonsus, Bishop

With Saint Ildefonsus, we celebrate Mary's willingness to accept God's will no matter what this obedience cost her.

Today is the Birthday of:

_____

_____

_____

Today is the Anniversary of:

_____

_____

Prayer: *Father, I give thanks for Your Church on earth which was ably served by St. Ildefonsus and is protected by our Mother Mary.*

JANUARY 24th

St. Francis de Sales

Whether laity or clergy, we are all blessed with certain gifts and responsibilities in serving our neighbors.

Today is the Birthday of:

Today is the Anniversary of:

Prayer: *Loving God, like Saint Francis de Sales, may I accept both my duties and my sanctification as Your child ready to do Your work.*

JANUARY 25th

The Conversion of St. Paul

God turned Paul onto a right path from a wrong path; we invite God to correct our direction when necessary.

Today is the Birthday of:

Today is the Anniversary of:

Prayer: *All-knowing Lord, You alone know what is best for me; let me welcome all opportunities You send to follow You even when it is difficult.*

JANUARY 26th

Sts. Timothy and Titus

We may often learn as much from those who convert to Christianity as we can from those born into Christianity.

Today is the Birthday of:

_____

_____

_____

Today is the Anniversary of:

_____

_____

Prayer: *God of All, like Sts. Timothy and Titus I pray to be open to everyone who can lead me closer to You.*

JANUARY 27th

St. Angela Merici

Like Saint Angela we look beyond the rules and conventions of our time and religion to forge new paths to God.

Today is the Birthday of:

Today is the Anniversary of:

Prayer: *Father, let me not be trapped by the institutions and routines of my life; let me see through to Your shining will and way.*

JANUARY 28th

St. Thomas Aquinas

Despite his brilliant writing and preaching, Saint Thomas Aquinas provides a model of humility for us to follow in this prideful world.

❧ ❧ ❧

Today is the Birthday of:

Today is the Anniversary of:

Prayer: *Lord, teach me all that a mere human can know about You, and then like Thomas Aquinas, let me never lose sight of how small I am and how great You are.*

JANUARY 29th

St. Gildas the Wise

Like Saint Gildas, even as we enjoy God's gifts, we remain vigilant and renounce the immoralities and cruelties of the world.

Today is the Birthday of:

Today is the Anniversary of:

Prayer: *Beloved Creator, help me recognize the many wrongs and evils in the world, and let me speak out and struggle against them.*

JANUARY 30th

St. Bathildis

Just as we avoid slavery to sin, we also try to free those who are enslaved by themselves or others.

❦   ❦   ❦

Today is the Birthday of:

Today is the Anniversary of:

Prayer: *Lord, I pray to learn from Saint Bathildis to practice self-denial and seek freedom for others.*

JANUARY 31st

St. Marcella

Choosing life as a widow to a new marriage, St. Marcella incurred public disdain to do God's work.

Today is the Birthday of:

Today is the Anniversary of:

Prayer: *Father, please give me the courage to make You and Your people my priority.*

The fear of the Lord

is the beginning

of wisdom.

Proverbs 9:10

FEBRUARY 1st

St. Brigid of Ireland

We strive to be generous with our time and talent, and like St. Brigid to serve others with joy and energy.

Today is the Birthday of:

Today is the Anniversary of:

Prayer: *Lord, help me in my actions to "show" You to people as much as "tell" them about You.*

FEBRUARY 2nd

Bl. Stephen Bellesini

Like Blessed Stephen Bellesini, when we encounter obstacles and disappointments in our faith journey, we will persevere and remain faithful to God's call.

Today is the Birthday of:

Today is the Anniversary of:

Prayer: *Jesus, please grant me the fortitude to keep trying when I meet with problems and frustrations.*

FEBRUARY 3rd

Sts. Simeon and Anna

With Saints Simeon and Anna, we wait upon the Lord, and then rejoice in His glorious presence.

Today is the Birthday of:

Today is the Anniversary of:

Prayer: *Father, I thank You for allowing me to know Your Son now and for the rest of my life.*

FEBRUARY 4th

St. Veronica

We welcome opportunities to "wipe the face of Jesus" by helping the poor, the hungry, and the suffering in our world.

Today is the Birthday of:

Today is the Anniversary of:

Prayer: *Lord, may Veronica's courageous example strengthen my resolve to seek Your face in everyone I meet.*

FEBRUARY 5th

St. Agatha, Martyr

February's flower, the violet, symbolizes the modesty and purity of St. Agatha, Patroness of Nurses, which we seek to demonstrate in our lives.

Today is the Birthday of:

_____

_____

_____

Today is the Anniversary of:

_____

_____

Prayer: *Faithful God, help me to follow Saint Agatha's example in dedicating my whole heart, mind, and body to You and Your people.*

FEBRUARY 6th

St. Paul Miki and Companions, Martyrs

Awestruck at the selflessness of the lay people and clergy who sacrificed everything, we try to be worthy to follow them.

Today is the Birthday of:

_____

_____

Today is the Anniversary of:

_____

_____

Prayer: *Father, help us to imitate the inclusive love You showed to the Japanese Saint, Paul Miki, and his companions from all over the world.*

FEBRUARY 7th

St. Moses

In bringing peace and God's word to the ancient Middle East, St. Moses gives us hope for that still-troubled region.

Today is the Birthday of:

Today is the Anniversary of:

Prayer: *Omniscient God, in the face of global war and terrorism, help me to be heartened by the knowledge that You make all things possible.*

FEBRUARY 8th

St. Stephen of Muret

Just as Saint Stephen of Muret's vocation resulted from illness, we search for God's plan for us in seeming setbacks.

Today is the Birthday of:

Today is the Anniversary of:

Prayer: *Trustworthy Lord, remind me that Your strength always overcomes my weakness if I submit myself to You.*

FEBRUARY 9th

St. Miguel Cordero

We pause to offer thanks for the glorious gift of the sacraments and those who like Saint Miguel Cordero prepare us to receive them.

Today is the Birthday of:

_____

_____

_____

Today is the Anniversary of:

_____

_____

Prayer: *I pray to experience the joy and innocence of a child when I gratefully receive the sacraments.*

FEBRUARY 10th

St. Scholastica

We work to build God's community of faith guided by the example of St. Scholastica and her brother, St. Benedict.

Today is the Birthday of:

_____

_____

Today is the Anniversary of:

_____

_____

r: I pray for the patience and 'o work within my own family greater love for God.

FEBRUARY 11th

Our Lady of Lourdes

We take heart in knowing that Jesus and His Blessed Mother speak to us in miraculous, amazing ways.

ஐ   ஐ   ஐ

Today is the Birthday of:

Today is the Anniversary of:

Prayer: *Jesus, beloved Son of Mary, You allow Your mother to intercede for all believers; help me to be open to her help in my life.*

FEBRUARY 12th

Bl. Humbeline

Like Blessed Humbeline, we seek freedom from the attachment to wealth and status that separates us from God.

Today is the Birthday of:

Today is the Anniversary of:

Prayer: *Lord, help me to loosen my grip on my possessions and position in the world and open my arms to You.*

FEBRUARY 13th

Bl. Christine of Spoleto

We strive to change whatever will make us more like Christ, even our very identities.

Today is the Birthday of:

Today is the Anniversary of:

Prayer: *Loving Christ, help me to imitate Blessed Christine who was so devoted to You that she even changed her name to be more like Yours.*

FEBRUARY 14th

St. Valentine, Martyr

We recognize and admire Saint Valentine's expression of the truest love: that of giving one's life for the Lord.

Today is the Birthday of:

Today is the Anniversary of:

Prayer: *Father, help me to love You, the Lord my God with all my strength, and to love others as I love myself.*

FEBRUARY 15th

St. Onesimus, Martyr

We are inspired by the humility of Saint Onesimus, first a slave, then a student and servant of Saint Paul.

Today is the Birthday of:

Today is the Anniversary of:

Prayer: *Lord Jesus, make me willing to be both servant and student to those who can bring me closer to You.*

FEBRUARY 16th

St. Maruthas

Saint Maruthas, diplomat, writer, bishop, and Father of the Syrian Church, shows us the many ways we can serve God and others.

Today is the Birthday of:

Today is the Anniversary of:

Prayer: *God of all resources, help me to be always ready to find a way to do Your work and draw others to You.*

FEBRUARY 17th

St. Fintan of Cloneehagh

St. Fintan's self-denial demonstrates that "less is more" when it comes to indulging appetites at the expense of devotion to God.

Today is the Birthday of:

Today is the Anniversary of:

Prayer: *Jesus, help me to temper my desires and appetites so that I can be "hungry" for You.*

FEBRUARY 18th

St. Theotonius

Outspoken in condemning vice and worldliness, Saint Theotonius teaches us to be generous in our abundance.

Today is the Birthday of:

Today is the Anniversary of:

Prayer: *Lord, help me to be like Saint Theotonius, who constantly gave alms to the poor; let me avoid greed and the hoarding of wealth.*

FEBRUARY 19th

Bl. Conrad of Piacenza

For our own sakes and the good of others, we must be ready always to confess our sins and to make restitution whenever possible.

Today is the Birthday of:

Today is the Anniversary of:

Prayer: *Father, give me the courage of Blessed Conrad, who confessed and paid for his thoughtless sin, saving a man's life in the process.*

FEBRUARY 20th

St. Eucherius

From Saint Eucherius, who surrendered the solitude he treasured, we learn the true blessing of obedience to Your Holy Will.

Today is the Birthday of:

Today is the Anniversary of:

Prayer: *Teaching God, please enlighten and enkindle my mind and heart when I read scripture.*

FEBRUARY 21st

Bl. Noel Pinot, Martyr

Blessed Noel Pinot's martyrdom reveals that even governments should be defied if they try to separate us from God.

Today is the Birthday of:

Today is the Anniversary of:

Prayer: *Jesus, Lord, please make me brave enough to espouse and practice Your teachings in the face of leaders who do not.*

FEBRUARY 22nd

Chair of St. Peter, Apostle

By choosing Peter to lead His Church, Jesus showed us that perfect faith is both a process and a gift.

Today is the Birthday of:

Today is the Anniversary of:

Prayer: *Lord, help me to learn from my mistakes and blunders, as St. Peter did, so that I can spend my life drawing ever closer to You.*

FEBRUARY 23rd

St. Polycarp

Just as Saint Polycarp worked to end division in the Church, we seek to heal and not hurt fellow Christians whose ideas differ from our own.

Today is the Birthday of:

Today is the Anniversary of:

Prayer: *Healing Father, show me how to appreciate the contributions of all who believe in You so that I may embody love and not division.*

FEBRUARY 24th

Bl. Josepha Naval Girbes

We learn from Bl. Josepha, a Third Order Carmelite, that we all have an important role to play in promoting the power of prayer.

Today is the Birthday of:

Today is the Anniversary of:

Prayer: *Almighty God, by being faithful to prayer and by encouraging others to pray, may I be an effective member of the laity.*

FEBRUARY 25th

St. Walburga

An abbess for both men and women, Saint Walburga reveals how God equips men and women for leadership roles.

༺❀༻   ༺❀༻   ༺❀༻

Today is the Birthday of:

_____

_____

_____

Today is the Anniversary of:

_____

_____

Prayer: *Father, help me to recognize and embrace the role You reserve for me and to be content with the roles You give others, regardless of gender.*

FEBRUARY 26th

St. Porphyrius

Through Saint Porphyrius, keeper of the Holy Cross, we are reminded of how essential the cross is in our faith.

Today is the Birthday of:

Today is the Anniversary of:

Prayer: *Suffering Jesus, let me never lose sight of what You sacrificed for me, and let that constant knowledge inform my life.*

FEBRUARY 27th

St. Anne Line, Martyr

Providing hospitality and service within our Church communities is a fulfilling way to demonstrate our love of God.

Today is the Birthday of:

Today is the Anniversary of:

Prayer: *Holy Spirit, I pray to be renewed daily in my faith and commitment to God and to those who serve the Church.*

FEBRUARY 28th

St. Romanus

Like Saint Romanus, we should take time to pray, meditate, read spiritual works and appreciate God's natural world.

Today is the Birthday of:

Today is the Anniversary of:

Prayer: *Father, help me to practice the simple disciplines of my faith, especially when the "world" becomes too overwhelming or demanding.*

FEBRUARY 29th

St. Hilary

By learning more about our faith, we can reject the false prophets and heresies in the Church as Pope Hilary did.

ಲಾಲ   ಲಾಲ   ಲಾಲ

Today is the Birthday of:

_____

_____

_____

Today is the Anniversary of:

_____

_____

Prayer: *I pray for the knowledge and wisdom to recognize and avoid religious falsehoods in my life.*

For God all things are possible.

Mark 10:27

MARCH 1st

St. Albinus

Saint Albinus reminds us that just as our minds and spirits should be given over to God, so should our bodies.

᭯   ᭯   ᭯

Today is the Birthday of:

Today is the Anniversary of:

Prayer: *Creator God, let me be conscious each day of devoting my every sense to recognizing Your presence.*

MARCH 2nd

Bl. Charles the Good, Martyr

Blessed Charles proves that we can do God's work by promoting honesty and charity in ourselves and others.

❧ ❧ ❧

Today is the Birthday of:

_____

_____

_____

Today is the Anniversary of:

_____

_____

Prayer: *Lord, lead me to grasp the opportunities You provide for me to model fairness and generosity both within and outside of Church.*

MARCH 3rd

St. Katharine Drexel

Like Saint Katharine, we stand against bigotry in all forms wherever we encounter it, whether in our communities or churches.

Today is the Birthday of:

Today is the Anniversary of:

Prayer: *Jesus, cleanse me of prejudice and let me be a friend to those who are persecuted and discriminated against.*

MARCH 4th

Bl. Placida Viel

Like March's flower, the daffodil, Bl. Placida demonstrated affection and cheerfulness as she educated poor girls in France.

Today is the Birthday of:

Today is the Anniversary of:

Prayer: *Father, help me to embody good cheer and kindness as I teach others about You.*

MARCH 5th

St. Virgil

Saint Virgil teaches us to support our churches through prayer, work and money.

Today is the Birthday of:

Today is the Anniversary of:

Prayer: *Jesus, help me to be creative and generous in sharing my time and talent with my local church.*

MARCH 6th

St. Chrodegang

With Saint Chrodegang who helped bring us the movingly beautiful Gregorian Chant, we celebrate our faith and love for God.

Today is the Birthday of:

Today is the Anniversary of:

Prayer: *I pray to appreciate the many forms of worship enhanced by music, art, and writing with which God has gifted us.*

MARCH 7th

Sts. Perpetua and Felicity, Martyrs

Though we can hardly imagine giving as much for our faith, Saints Perpetua and Felicity inspire us to greater sacrifice.

Today is the Birthday of:

Today is the Anniversary of:

Prayer: *Jesus, awestruck by those who gave their lives for You, I pray for the strength to give even a fraction of what they gave.*

MARCH 8th

St. John of God

Shepherd, soldier, Patron of Booksellers, Saint John of God demonstrates that we can undergo transformation throughout our life.

Today is the Birthday of:

_____

_____

_____

Today is the Anniversary of:

_____

_____

Prayer: *Merciful Father, please don't let my sins, failings, and confusion blind me to the light You shine on my proper path.*

MARCH 9th

St. Frances of Rome

We understand from Saint Frances that we can serve God through many roles in family and religious life.

Today is the Birthday of:

Today is the Anniversary of:

Prayer: *Lord, show me that there are many paths which lead to You, and help me to be open to walking more than one in my lifetime.*

MARCH 10th

St. John Ogilvie, Martyr

Saint John Ogilvie reveals that conversion as a thoughtful process is as valid as conversion through our emotions.

Today is the Birthday of:

Today is the Anniversary of:

Prayer: *Jesus, let me never take my closeness to You for granted, for it is only when I am aware of You in my life that I can bring others to You.*

MARCH 11th

St. Eulogius, Martyr

The life and martyrdom of Saint Eulogius reminds us how effective prayer-based action is in building the Kingdom of God.

Today is the Birthday of:

Today is the Anniversary of:

Prayer: *Jesus, You taught us how to pray to the Father; please remind me to use the words You gave us often and with deep sincerity.*

MARCH 12th

Bl. Seraphina

Blessed Seraphina provides a model for how to use physical suffering and humiliation to advance our spiritual growth.

Today is the Birthday of:

Today is the Anniversary of:

Prayer: *Suffering Jesus, help me to bear my aches, pains, and illnesses by keeping an image of Your suffering always in my mind and heart.*

MARCH 13th

⤳⤲

St. Leander of Seville

It is due to St. Leander that we reflect on the glorious mystery of our faith, the Holy Trinity, when we proclaim the Creed at Mass.

Today is the Birthday of:

Today is the Anniversary of:

Prayer: *Loving God, I pray that You give me the intelligence and discernment to know You as Father, Son, and Holy Spirit.*

MARCH 14th

St. Mathilda

Patroness of queens, Saint Mathilda proves that political leaders can encourage charity through righteous leadership.

Today is the Birthday of:

Today is the Anniversary of:

Prayer: *Lord, I thank You for those leaders who model and promote Christianity in government.*

MARCH 15th

St. Louise De Marillac

As a widow, Saint Louise exemplified service to the poor and sick, an example we should follow as Jesus taught.

Today is the Birthday of:

Today is the Anniversary of:

Prayer: *Healing Jesus, give me a generous, fearless spirit so that I may follow Your command to love.*

MARCH 16th

St. Eusebia

We learn through Saint Eusebia that youth is no impediment to righteousness and that God may communicate through the young.

Today is the Birthday of:

Today is the Anniversary of:

Prayer: *Father, thank You for showing me that wisdom can be found in the very young as well as the very old . . . and anyone in between.*

MARCH 17th

St. Patrick, Apostle of Ireland

Saint Patrick teaches us that we can turn things that imprison us into things that free us by embracing God's will.

Today is the Birthday of:

Today is the Anniversary of:

Prayer: *Jesus, when I feel enslaved by events or people in my life, remind me that I need only turn to You to find freedom and hope.*

MARCH 18th

St. Cyril of Jerusalem

St. Cyril's success in upholding the unity of the early Church teaches us to trust in the work of the Holy Spirit.

Today is the Birthday of:

Today is the Anniversary of:

Prayer: *Righteous God, give me the courage of my convictions when my convictions are based in You.*

MARCH 19th

∽∽∽

St. Joseph, Husband of Mary

Saint Joseph, foster father to Jesus, reveals how wondrously God rewards a simple, dignified life of obedience.

Today is the Birthday of:

Today is the Anniversary of:

Prayer: *Jesus, help me to give tribute to kind and humble parents who sacrifice so much.*

MARCH 20th

St. Cuthbert

Ministering to animals as a shepherd and to people as a bishop, Saint Cuthbert teaches us to care for all God's creatures.

Today is the Birthday of:

Today is the Anniversary of:

Prayer: *Creator God, let me embrace every living creature in Your love.*

MARCH 21st

St. Nicholas of Flue

Husband, father, diplomat, hermit, Saint Nicholas leads us to use our God-given skills wherever and however they are needed.

Today is the Birthday of:

Today is the Anniversary of:

Prayer: *Kind Father, reveal to me how I may use my talents for Your glory, praise, and honor.*

MARCH 22nd

St. Nicholas of Owen, Martyr

We seek to follow the example of Saint Nicholas by protecting and cherishing all good and righteous clergy.

Today is the Birthday of:

Today is the Anniversary of:

Prayer: *Righteous God, remind me that judgment belongs to You alone and help me avoid gossip, accusations, and meanness.*

MARCH 23rd

St. Walter of Pontoise

Saint Walter reminds us that honors and titles mean nothing if we don't have our hearts and spirits set on God.

Today is the Birthday of:

Today is the Anniversary of:

Prayer: *Lord, teach me to strive for the honors and titles that please You and to use my power to fight injustice.*

MARCH 24th

St. Catherine of Sweden

A strong faith and prayer life begins in the family, as with Saint Catherine, her husband, and her mother, Saint Bridget.

Today is the Birthday of:

_____

_____

_____

Today is the Anniversary of:

_____

_____

Prayer: *Father of all, may my family better devote themselves to You through common prayer, action, contemplation, and service.*

MARCH 25th

The Annunciation of the Lord

We venerate and love Mary because she bore Jesus, our Savior, and because she devoted her life to Him.

❦ ❦ ❦

Today is the Birthday of:

Today is the Anniversary of:

Prayer: *Blessed Mother, teach me to conform my will to God's will just as you did when you accepted the message of the Angel Gabriel.*

MARCH 26th

St. Castulus

From Saint Castulus we learn to use what worldly powers we hold to promote faith and acts of Christianity.

Today is the Birthday of:

Today is the Anniversary of:

Prayer: *Father, lead me to use my influence to protect, practice, and nurture my faith and the faith of every Christian I meet.*

MARCH 27th

Bl. Peregrine of Falerone

Just as Blessed Peregrine was inspired by Saint Francis of Assisi, we seek those who follow God to inspire us.

Today is the Birthday of:

_____

_____

Today is the Anniversary of:

_____

_____

Prayer: *Merciful Father, send me people who will lead me closer to You; help me to recognize and willingly learn from them.*

MARCH 28th

St. Stephen Harding

Like Saint Stephen, we search always for opportunities to reform and organize our lives around the truths of the Gospels.

Today is the Birthday of:

Today is the Anniversary of:

Prayer: *Jesus, Your words in the Gospels tell me exactly how to live; open my heart and mind to embrace and form my life around them.*

MARCH 29th

~~~

St. Mark

Saint Mark teaches us that by loving our enemies, we may affect their conversion through our example of Christianity.

Today is the Birthday of:

Today is the Anniversary of:

Prayer: *Jesus, Rabbi, too often I want to hurt those who hurt me; give me the strength to show my enemies the love that may bring them to You.*

MARCH 30th

St. John Climacus

We learn from Saint John Climacus that silence both in solitude and community can indicate a heart devoted to God.

ം ം ം

Today is the Birthday of:

Today is the Anniversary of:

Prayer: *God, when I am astounded by Your majesty and creation, remind me that my silent gratitude is an acceptable expression and gift to You.*

MARCH 31st

Bl. Joan of Toulouse

Blessed Joan shows that even when we have little to give, we must help those who are less fortunate than we are.

Today is the Birthday of:

Today is the Anniversary of:

Prayer: *Jesus, help me to stretch myself to be more generous to the poor and needy, even when it means I must do without.*

If you wish to

enter into life,

keep the commandments.

Matthew 19:17

APRIL 1st

St. Hugh of Grenoble

Through Saint Hugh we are reminded that doing God's work can sometimes be hard and tedious, requiring perseverance.

Today is the Birthday of:

_____

_____

Today is the Anniversary of:

_____

Prayer: *Father, give me the fortitude to take on the work of faith-building even when it is less than exciting and requires deep and lasting effort.*

APRIL 2nd

St. Francis of Paola

We learn from St. Francis, who founded the Order of Minims, how small acts of kindness can influence the powerful to embrace God.

Today is the Birthday of:

Today is the Anniversary of:

Prayer: *Father, humble me so that I can be a channel of peace and hope in the world.*

APRIL 3rd

St. Nicetas

Saint Nicetas shows us the importance of keeping sacred images as reminders of our faith and love for God.

Today is the Birthday of:

Today is the Anniversary of:

Prayer: *Creator God, You move artists to create sacred images; help me to be inspired by them and to use them to increase my faith.*

APRIL 4th

St. Isidore of Seville

In Saint Isidore we see how science and great learning can be used to advance Christianity, discipline, and conversion.

Today is the Birthday of:

Today is the Anniversary of:

Prayer: *Lord, open my mind so that I can be ready to embrace all opportunities You provide to achieve greater knowledge of Your ways.*

APRIL 5th

St. Vincent Ferrer

Patron of Builders, Saint Vincent Ferrer's evangelistic zeal proves there are many ways for us to build and strengthen the Church.

Today is the Birthday of:

Today is the Anniversary of:

Prayer: *Jesus, teach me to build my life, and my work in faith, on the solid foundation that is You.*

APRIL 6th

St. Irenaeus of Sirmium

April's flower, the daisy, represents tenaciousness as did Saint Irenaeus who continually professed his faith even faced with torment and death.

Today is the Birthday of:

Today is the Anniversary of:

Prayer: *Father, give me the strength to be faithful even when I am confronted with mockery and fear.*

APRIL 7th

St. John Baptist De La Salle

As Patron of Teachers, Saint John shows us that teaching the poor is a noble, selfless act of Christianity.

Today is the Birthday of:

Today is the Anniversary of:

Prayer: *All-knowing God, thank You for every occasion You provide me to teach by example and to encourage all teachers.*

APRIL 8th

St. Julia Billiart

By founding the Sisters of Notre Dame, Saint Julia Billiart exemplifies love and support of the poor despite physical hardship.

Today is the Birthday of:

Today is the Anniversary of:

Prayer: *Lord, just as St. Julia defied those who disliked her modern ways, give me the courage to follow Your path when others try to dissuade me.*

APRIL 9th

St. Hugh of Rouen

We admire Saint Hugh for using his wealth and power to promote the faith and to help believers who had little or nothing.

❦ ❦ ❦

Today is the Birthday of:

Today is the Anniversary of:

Prayer: *Jesus, You taught that we must give to the poor; help me to realize that I need not be wealthy to share what I have.*

APRIL 10th

St. Fulbert

From Saint Fulbert we learn that early mentors in life can have a powerful influence on spiritual growth and learning.

Today is the Birthday of:

Today is the Anniversary of:

Prayer: *Father, give me the insight to know that I may do a great deal of good in Your name by mentoring and encouraging young people.*

APRIL 11th

St. Stanislaus, Martyr

Saint Stanislaus teaches us that we should be able to depend on Church leaders to oppose corrupt political leaders.

Today is the Birthday of:

Today is the Anniversary of:

Prayer: *Lord, give me the grace to support and assist all Church leaders who fight injustice, discrimination, and corruption in the world.*

APRIL 12th

St. Julius I

Like Saint Julius who succeeded St. Mark as pope in 337, we must try to heal divisions among people of faith.

Today is the Birthday of:

_____

_____

_____

Today is the Anniversary of:

_____

_____

Prayer: *Father, when divisions in the Church arise help me to promote unity in a loving, healing, peaceful manner.*

APRIL 13th

St. Hermenegild

Saint Hermenegild shows that our first bond must be to God and to reject family members who oppose God's will.

Today is the Birthday of:

Today is the Anniversary of:

Prayer: *Jesus, give me the strength to make Your commandments and Your will my objective no matter how it may strain my other relationships.*

APRIL 14th

St. Lydwina

Lydwina's peace with God after her tragic accident makes her a model for young people whose careers are cut short.

Today is the Birthday of:

Today is the Anniversary of:

Prayer: *Dear Father, help us, Your children, to turn our misfortunes and suffering into good for others.*

APRIL 15th

Bl. Cesar de Bus

From Blessed Cesar we learn to respect and support both men and women who devote their lives to spreading the faith.

Today is the Birthday of:

_____

_____

_____

Today is the Anniversary of:

_____

_____

Prayer: *Jesus, help me to celebrate all people, regardless of gender, who serve You and spread Your teachings.*

APRIL 16th

St. Marie Bernadette Soubirous

Saint Bernadette of Lourdes demonstrates that God may use the weakest among us to bring His healing message to the world.

Today is the Birthday of:

Today is the Anniversary of:

Prayer: *Father, open my heart and my mind to all miracles and apparitions sent from You so that I may rejoice in Your everlasting love.*

APRIL 17th

St. Robert of Molesmes

Saint Robert reminds us that reform, whether of ourselves or our Church, is accomplished through our cooperation with God's grace.

Today is the Birthday of:

Today is the Anniversary of:

Prayer: *Righteous God, give me the fortitude and perseverance to remove all obstacles in my path to You.*

APRIL 18th

St. Athanasia

We learn from Saint Athanasia that whether married or single, we can discern and accomplish God's will for ourselves and others.

Today is the Birthday of:

Today is the Anniversary of:

Prayer: *Father, I offer myself, in whatever my current situation is, to You; please make me an instrument of Your will.*

APRIL 19th

St. Leo IX

Through Saint Leo, a reform-minded pope who traveled frequently, we learn to seek God's Kingdom throughout the world.

Today is the Birthday of:

Today is the Anniversary of:

Prayer: *Jesus, give me the courage to follow in Your footsteps wherever they may lead me in Your service.*

APRIL 20th

St. Marcellinus

Saint Marcellinus proves that we must spend time in both prayer and active ministry to be well-rounded Christians.

Today is the Birthday of:

Today is the Anniversary of:

Prayer: *Father, when I am "doing" remind me to never neglect praying; and through my praying, teach me what I should be "doing."*

APRIL 21st

St. Anselm

From Saint Anselm's extensive writing we see the need to know more about our faith.

Today is the Birthday of:

Today is the Anniversary of:

Prayer: *Always-present God, let me rejoice so utterly in Your presence that I can easily withstand the doubters of the world.*

APRIL 22nd

Sts. Epepodius and Alexander, Martyrs

Saints Epepodius and Alexander teach us that friends in faith can help and encourage one another in all circumstances.

Today is the Birthday of:

Today is the Anniversary of:

Prayer: *Lord, bring into my life friends who will support me in my faith and who will be my stalwart companions on the road to You.*

APRIL 23rd

Bl. Helen of Udine

Through her silence Blessed Helen exemplifies the need for us to be quiet so that we can hear the voice of God.

Today is the Birthday of:

Today is the Anniversary of:

Prayer: *Soft-spoken Father, help me to seek and to spend silent time with You to listen and receive Your words.*

APRIL 24th

Sts. Mary of Cleophas and Salome

Blessed by knowing Jesus, Saints Mary and Salome show us that all worldly things amount to nothing in His presence.

Today is the Birthday of:

Today is the Anniversary of:

Prayer: *Risen Jesus, let me, like the women who followed You, devote myself single-mindedly to You.*

APRIL 25th

St. Mark, Evangelist

Writer of a gospel, Saint Mark revealed Jesus to early Church converts, and we strive to do the same in our day.

Today is the Birthday of:

Today is the Anniversary of:

Prayer: *Jesus, show me how to reveal You to the world and affect conversion through my thoughts, my words, my actions, my work.*

APRIL 26th

St. Paschasius Radbertus

Saint Paschasius' abiding love for the Holy Eucharist demonstrates how vital it is for us to receive Christ's body and blood.

Today is the Birthday of:

_____

_____

_____

Today is the Anniversary of:

_____

_____

Prayer: *Giving Lord, I rejoice in the opportunity to receive You, and thus join myself to You and to Christians everywhere.*

APRIL 27th

St. Zita

Patroness of Domestic Workers, Saint Zita elevates the role of servant and illustrates the connection between work and piety.

Today is the Birthday of:

_____

_____

_____

Today is the Anniversary of:

_____

_____

Prayer: *Jesus, help me to be content with my role as a worker and empathetic in all my dealings with other workers.*

APRIL 28th

St. Pamphilus

As a bishop Saint Pamphilus demonstrated that love of the poor and appreciation of Liturgy bring balance to our lives.

Today is the Birthday of:

Today is the Anniversary of:

Prayer: *Beloved Lord, through our devotion to the Eucharist may we bless the world and those in it.*

APRIL 29th

St. Catherine of Siena

A brilliant theologian, Saint Catherine teaches us that seeking God also involves seeking peace and unity in the Church.

Today is the Birthday of:

Today is the Anniversary of:

Prayer: *Almighty God, let me devote my mind to learning about You, my heart to loving You and Your people, and my body to serving You.*

APRIL 30th

St. Joseph Cottolengo

Saint Joseph shows us that we must support homeless shelters, group homes, and residences for the poor, ill, and troubled.

Today is the Birthday of:

_____

_____

_____

Today is the Anniversary of:

_____

_____

Prayer: *Jesus, when I am afraid to "get involved" in helping the "least of my brethren," remind me that to follow You I must aid them . . . all of them.*

Your friends must be loved for My sake.

Bk. 3, 42.
Imitation of Christ

MAY 1st

St. Peregrine Laziosi

By converting when someone "turned the other cheek" to him, Saint Peregrine embodies for us the importance of repentance.

Today is the Birthday of:

Today is the Anniversary of:

Prayer: *Lord, help me to forgive those who hurt me and to seek opportunities to move others to forgiveness.*

MAY 2nd

St. Wiborada, Martyr

By accepting from God the gift of prophecy, Saint Wiborada reminds us that God does indeed move in gloriously mysterious ways.

Today is the Birthday of:

Today is the Anniversary of:

Prayer: *Father, I thank You for communicating with me in ways, both ordinary and extraordinary; help me to always listen.*

MAY 3rd

Sts. Philip and James, Apostles

We are blessed that Saints Philip and James both taught and wrote about Jesus, so that we too may know Him.

Today is the Birthday of:

Today is the Anniversary of:

Prayer: *Jesus, I praise You always for men and women who made You known to the world; let me never tire of learning about You.*

MAY 4th

St. Florian, Martyr

Saint Florian, a soldier, demonstrates that we may find Christians devoted to God in every profession and "walk of life."

Today is the Birthday of:

Today is the Anniversary of:

Prayer: *Lord, protect all those who serve in the military and help me to see Your face in everyone I meet.*

MAY 5th

St. Gothard

Saint Gothard, who built churches and schools, reminds us not to forget those who are sick and dying.

Today is the Birthday of:

Today is the Anniversary of:

Prayer: *Healing Jesus, help me to make the time to visit and assist those who are lonely and ill.*

MAY 6th

St. Peter Nolasco

Just as Saint Peter Nolasco rescued slaves, we must try to help those enslaved by addiction, poverty, and abuse.

Today is the Birthday of:

Today is the Anniversary of:

Prayer: *Watchful God, give me the grace and courage to seek freedom from all that enslaves me.*

MAY 7th

Bl. Gisele

We know through Blessed Gisele, a widow and mother, that we can nurture devotion to God in those we love.

Today is the Birthday of:

Today is the Anniversary of:

Prayer: *Father, help me to be the kind of parent, spouse, friend, and even stranger who shows people their potential to serve You.*

MAY 8th

St. Desideratus

Saint Desideratus embodies the adage, "charity begins at home," and we seek to model charity in our families and communities.

Today is the Birthday of:

Today is the Anniversary of:

Prayer: *Lord, by being generous and charitable myself, help me to teach those around me to be giving and caring individuals.*

MAY 9th

St. Isaiah, Prophet

Isaiah's life and glorious prophecies about Jesus teach us to attend to the holy, just men and women in today's world.

Today is the Birthday of:

Today is the Anniversary of:

Prayer: *All-knowing God, direct me to reach out in love to those You have sent as prophets.*

MAY 10th

St. Damien Joseph de Veuster

Saint Damien, through his gentle and dedicated care of lepers on Molokai, shows us that we can heal others in God's name.

Today is the Birthday of:

_____

_____

_____

Today is the Anniversary of:

_____

_____

Prayer: *Healing God, open my heart and hands to bring comfort to the sick and dying both near and far.*

MAY 11th

St. Francis di Girolamo

Saint Francis' reputation as a good confessor reminds us of the necessity and grace of confession and repentance.

Today is the Birthday of:

Today is the Anniversary of:

Prayer: *Lord, give me the courage to come to Your Sacrament and confess my sins, knowing that if I am sincere, You will forgive and cleanse me.*

MAY 12th

St. Pancras, Martyr

Saint Pancras' wholehearted charity and fidelity to God inspires us to proclaim our faith as God's children and to give alms.

Today is the Birthday of:

Today is the Anniversary of:

Prayer: *Father, I pray for those all over the world who are threatened with oppression, imprisonment, and even death for their faith and charity.*

MAY 13th

Our Lady of Fatima

Through Mary's visitations and our prayers and devotion to her, we are reminded of the power of intercessory prayer.

Today is the Birthday of:

Today is the Anniversary of:

Prayer: *Beloved Lord Jesus, I pray that You hear the intercessions of Your mother Mary and all the Saints on behalf of our troubled world.*

MAY 14th

St. Matthias, Apostle

May's flower, the lily of the valley, represents the return of happiness granted to the apostles when Matthias was chosen to replace Judas.

Today is the Birthday of:

Today is the Anniversary of:

Prayer: *Lord, when I am discouraged, remind me that You always have a plan and a wonderful resolution may be right around the corner.*

MAY 15th

St. Isidore

Patron of Farmers, Saint Isidore reminds us to be grateful for God's bounty and those who nurture and harvest it.

Today is the Birthday of:

Today is the Anniversary of:

Prayer: *Lord of all creation, I ask Your blessing on all those who work the earth and keep the flocks that feed and nourish the world.*

MAY 16th

∽∽∽

St. Brendan

Patron of Sailors, Saint Brendan demonstrates to us that when we travel with God, we travel without fear.

Today is the Birthday of:

Today is the Anniversary of:

Prayer: *God Who sees all paths, make me brave enough to pursue even the stormy seas that will allow me to follow and serve You.*

MAY 17th

St. Restituta, Martyr

Through Saint Restituta, we remember that many great saints came from Africa—a stronghold of Christianity today.

Today is the Birthday of:

_____

_____

_____

Today is the Anniversary of:

_____

_____

Prayer: *Jesus, though You never traveled far in Your life on earth, I rejoice that faith in You has spread to every corner of the earth.*

MAY 18th

St. John I, Martyr

Saint John's negotiations as pope in a divisive time show us that too often the world favors politics over faith.

Today is the Birthday of:

_____

_____

_____

Today is the Anniversary of:

_____

_____

Prayer: *Father, help me to be a force for healing and peace rather than a mouthpiece for my own agenda.*

MAY 19th

St. Yves

Patron of Lawyers, Saint Yves demonstrated that the law of men is only valid when in keeping with the law of God.

Today is the Birthday of:

Today is the Anniversary of:

Prayer: *All-knowing God, teach me that all good and just laws have their foundation in Your laws and Your justice.*

MAY 20th

St. Bernardine of Siena

Patron of Advertisers, Saint Bernardine "advertised" the Christian life by his example and care of the sick, just as we should.

Today is the Birthday of:

Today is the Anniversary of:

Prayer: *Lord, I pray that I might be a good "advertisement" for Christian living, so that all who know me will know that I belong to You.*

MAY 21st

Sts. Christopher Magallanes and Companions, Martyrs

These martyrs who died in Mexico in the 20th century, demonstrate that even in modern times, we must defend our faith.

Today is the Birthday of:

Today is the Anniversary of:

Prayer: *Jesus, Lord, in these days of religious extremism and terrorism, I pray for an end to persecution and for an increase in acceptance and love.*

MAY 22nd

∽∾∾

St. Rita of Cascia

Patroness of Impossible Cases, Saint Rita shows that we must pray for all who seem lost or evil, and leave judgment to God.

❦   ❦   ❦

Today is the Birthday of:

_____

_____

_____

Today is the Anniversary of:

_____

_____

Prayer: *Almighty, all-seeing Father, turn my anger and unforgiveness into a sincere effort to pray for those who have hurt me or my loved ones.*

MAY 23rd

St. John Baptist Dei Rossi

Saint John teaches us to "practice what we preach" when it comes to helping the sick, poor, and homeless.

Today is the Birthday of:

Today is the Anniversary of:

Prayer: *Ministering Lord, help me to remember that it is not enough to talk about aiding those in need; I pray for the strength in order to do it.*

MAY 24th

St. Simeon Stylites the Younger

In Saint Simeon's hermitic lifestyle, we are reminded to strive to eliminate all ego and self-absorption in our relationship with God.

Today is the Birthday of:

Today is the Anniversary of:

Prayer: *Father, teach me to seek only Your regard and Your good opinion in all that I am and do.*

MAY 25th

St. Bede the Venerable

Saint Bede's brilliant studies and writings show us that no area of knowledge or science can be outside God's authority.

Today is the Birthday of:

Today is the Anniversary of:

Prayer: *Creator God, I thank You for making heaven and earth and all things in them and of them.*

MAY 26th

~~~

St. Philip Neri

Saint Philip exemplifies for us secondary obedience to our earthly parents and primary obedience to our divine Parent.

Today is the Birthday of:

_____

_____

Today is the Anniversary of:

_____

_____

Prayer: *Father God, I pray that You give wisdom and kindness to all who are in authority over me, so that I may obey You in obeying them.*

MAY 27th

St. Bruno of Wurzburg

Saint Bruno showed us that we may serve God in many ways from manual labor to academics to administration.

Today is the Birthday of:

_____

_____

_____

Today is the Anniversary of:

_____

_____

Prayer: *Father, develop in me the skills You have given me so that I may better serve You and those I meet according to Your plan.*

MAY 28th

St. Germanus

From Saint Germanus we learn to never cease in trying to influence government leaders to be peacemakers.

Today is the Birthday of:

Today is the Anniversary of:

Prayer: *God, give me a voice to proclaim Your ways and praise Your goodness to all leaders.*

MAY 29th

∽∞∾

St. Richard Thirkeld, Martyr

Saint Richard demonstrates that those who become committed to God later in life can often work wonders through their dedication.

༺ ༻   ༺ ༻   ༺ ༻

Today is the Birthday of:

_____

_____

_____

Today is the Anniversary of:

_____

_____

Prayer: *Father, thank You for drawing women and men to You regardless of age, race, background, or status.*

MAY 30th

St. Joan of Arc

Saint Joan proved that advanced scholarship or knowledge of religious rules are not necessary when a pure heart seeks God.

Today is the Birthday of:

Today is the Anniversary of:

Prayer: *Almighty God, please protect all the innocents in the world who seek You with a pure, full heart of love; and let me be among them.*

MAY 31st

St. Petronilla, Martyr

Saint Petronilla illustrates that no woman or man can dictate God's will to us if God Himself shows us another way.

Today is the Birthday of:

Today is the Anniversary of:

Prayer: *Beloved Father, silence the clamor of others who think they know best for me, so that I may hear Your direction, and only Yours.*

Without faith it is
impossible
to please God.

Hebrews 11:6

JUNE 1st

St. Justin, Martyr

Through Saint Justin, philosopher and apologist, we understand the meaning of truth and bearing witness to it.

Today is the Birthday of:

Today is the Anniversary of:

Prayer: *Jesus, give me the strength and the discernment to love truth and to be steadfast in my faith.*

JUNE 2nd

St. Erasmus, Martyr

Saint Erasmus, Patron of Sailors, reminds us that even in the midst of great difficulties and emergencies, God is our refuge.

Today is the Birthday of:

_____

_____

_____

Today is the Anniversary of:

_____

_____

Prayer: *All-guiding God, when I am afflicted, lost, afraid, lead from the darkness of fear and confusion into Your hope-filled light.*

JUNE 3rd

St. Clotilda, Queen

Saint Clotilda teaches that even when disappointed by or separated from our biological family, we may turn to our Christian family.

Today is the Birthday of:

_____

_____

_____

Today is the Anniversary of:

_____

_____

Prayer: *Father, help me to feel and act as a part of Your family, especially when I am unwillingly estranged from my earthly family.*

JUNE 4th

St. Francis Caracciolo

When we travel, we should emulate Saint Francis who used his pilgrimages to show the face and beauty of God to the poor and sick.

Today is the Birthday of:

Today is the Anniversary of:

Prayer: *Lord, wherever You lead me, let me never ignore a chance to bring word of Your love and care to those I encounter.*

JUNE 5th

St. Boniface, Martyr

Saint Boniface reminds us of Jesus' words that there is little merit in loving and helping only those who love us.

Today is the Birthday of:

_____

_____

_____

Today is the Anniversary of:

_____

_____

Prayer: *Jesus, help me to be brave enough to win the hearts and minds of those who do not yet believe in You.*

JUNE 6th

∽∽∽

St. Norbert

In Saint Norbert we remember to welcome the "bolts of lightning" that allow us to change and reform our lives.

☙ ☙ ☙

Today is the Birthday of:

_____

_____

_____

Today is the Anniversary of:

_____

_____

Prayer: *Father, I pray that it will not take a "lightning bolt" to awaken me to You, but if it does, let me embrace its saving power.*

JUNE 7th

Bl. Anne of Saint Bartholomew

In Blessed Anne's service to Saint Teresa and the Carmelites, we see the importance of a "supporting role."

Today is the Birthday of:

_____

_____

_____

Today is the Anniversary of:

_____

_____

Prayer: *All-consuming God, give me the presence of mind to put my ego aside and to serve You with simplicity.*

JUNE 8th

St. William of York

Saint William's unfair treatment shows that we can never know a person's heart and should not judge or gossip.

Today is the Birthday of:

Today is the Anniversary of:

Prayer: *Father, close my ears to gossip and rumor; close my lips to slander and cruelty; close my mind to unfair judgment and assumptions.*

JUNE 9th

St. Columba

Saint Columba and many other saints show how much help and comfort we give and receive as companions in faith.

Today is the Birthday of:

Today is the Anniversary of:

Prayer: *Lord, empower me through faithful companions and let me, in turn, lend them my strength and support at every opportunity.*

JUNE 10th

St. Landericus

By erecting one of the first hospitals for the poor in Paris, Saint Landericus embodied Jesus' command that we care for the sick.

Today is the Birthday of:

Today is the Anniversary of:

Prayer: *Father, fill me with compassion and motivate me to act to help all Your children, especially those who are poor and sick.*

JUNE 11th

St. Barnabas

An apostle whose very name means *exhortation* and *consolation*, Saint Barnabas teaches us to both encourage and comfort others.

Today is the Birthday of:

_____

_____

_____

Today is the Anniversary of:

_____

_____

Prayer: *Beloved God, do not let me become so enamored of preaching that I forget to act, or so blindly active that I forget to speak Your word.*

JUNE 12th

Bl. Guy Vignotelli of Cortona

Like St. Francis of Assisi, Bl. Guy followed Jesus' directive to sell his possessions, give to the poor, and follow Him.

Today is the Birthday of:

Today is the Anniversary of:

Prayer: *Jesus, make me generous, so that I may be lightened of my possessions enough to follow You.*

JUNE 13th

St. Anthony of Padua

Patron of those who have suffered a loss, Saint Anthony reminds us that none of us are lost to God.

Today is the Birthday of:

_____

_____

Today is the Anniversary of:

_____

_____

Prayer: *Father, help me to believe that even when I feel vulnerable and alone, I am not lost to You for You always wait for me with open arms.*

JUNE 14th

St. Elisha, Prophet

Like June's flowery symbol of strength, the rose, Elisha showed Israel God's strength through miracles and prophecies.

Today is the Birthday of:

Today is the Anniversary of:

Prayer: *God, open my heart and mind to the wonders worked and spoken by Your prophets of old and Your prophets of today.*

JUNE 15th

St. Germaine Cousin

The comfort and joy Saint Germaine received from daily Mass and the Rosary recommend those powerful rituals to us.

Today is the Birthday of:

_____

_____

_____

Today is the Anniversary of:

_____

_____

Prayer: *Lord, let me focus myself on You by partaking in the Eucharist and reciting the Rosary often.*

JUNE 16th

St. Lutgardis

We are inspired to be holy by Saint Lutgardis, who God gifted with powers of visions, prophecy and healing.

Today is the Birthday of:

_____

_____

_____

Today is the Anniversary of:

_____

_____

Prayer: *God of all gifts, help me to recognize, appreciate, and use all my gifts to do Your will.*

JUNE 17th

St. Theresa of Portugal

Queen, mother, and saint, Theresa shows that our most important title must always be that of Christian, ready for God's work.

∽∾∽   ∽∾∽   ∽∾∽

Today is the Birthday of:

_____

_____

Today is the Anniversary of:

_____

_____

Prayer: *Father, teach me that the work You've given me must cut across all boundaries and shatter all the limits of my lesser roles.*

JUNE 18th

Bl. Osanna of Mantua

Blessed Osanna's visions and experiences of Christ's suffering remind us never to forget what Jesus endured for us.

Today is the Birthday of:

Today is the Anniversary of:

Prayer: *Suffering Jesus, give me the strength not only to think about Your suffering, but to make it the focus of my devotion to You.*

JUNE 19th

St. Juliana Falconieri

We seek to imitate the selflessness of Saint Juliana whose commitment to serving God led her to found a religious order.

Today is the Birthday of:

Today is the Anniversary of:

Prayer: *Generous God, I thank You for all those holy men and women who established communities that continue to serve Your people today.*

JUNE 20th

St. John of Matera

The victim of jealousy, Saint John inspires us in the way he continued his service despite false charges and envy.

Today is the Birthday of:

Today is the Anniversary of:

Prayer: *Lord, when I am the target of jealousy and lies, encourage me to walk with You until the truth is known.*

JUNE 21st

St. Aloysius Gonzaga

In his youthful devotion and early death, Saint Aloysius demonstrates that faith and wisdom are gifts of God, not of age.

Today is the Birthday of:

Today is the Anniversary of:

Prayer: *Father, prepare me to respect and affirm all Your children of every age and race.*

JUNE 22nd

∽∽∽

St. Paulinus of Nola

Saint Paulinus' reputation as a Christian poet reminds us that there are many ways to creatively express our faith.

Today is the Birthday of:

Today is the Anniversary of:

Prayer: *Creator God, move me to demonstrate my devotion to You in all ways, both practical and poetical.*

JUNE 23rd

Bl. Mary of Oignies

Blessed Mary's counsel and direction to others reminds us that God sends us advisors and helpers in our journey to Him.

Today is the Birthday of:

Today is the Anniversary of:

Prayer: *Lord, help me to recognize, heed, and appreciate those You've sent to inspire, counsel, and direct me.*

JUNE 24th

Nativity of St. John the Baptist

We are in awe of John the Baptist, who recognized Jesus before birth and willingly followed Him to death.

Today is the Birthday of:

Today is the Anniversary of:

Prayer: *Jesus, help me to practice selfless dedication to You, so that like John, I can try to prepare the world to receive You.*

JUNE 25th

St. Prosper of Reggio

In his generous charity Saint Prosper reminds us that we can only truly prosper when we help others prosper.

Today is the Birthday of:

_____

_____

_____

Today is the Anniversary of:

_____

_____

Prayer: *Father, help me to be willing to use the gifts You have given me to help others.*

JUNE 26th

St. Josemaria Escriva de Balaguer

We seek to follow Saint Josemaria's motto: "to hide and disappear (our egos and pride) so that only Jesus may shine."

Today is the Birthday of:

Today is the Anniversary of:

Prayer: *Jesus, Lord, teach me to live my life in humility while working for the glory and praise of Your name.*

JUNE 27th

St. Cyril of Alexandria

Through Saint Cyril's tireless work, we proclaim that Jesus was truly the Son of God from the moment of His conception.

Today is the Birthday of:

_____

_____

_____

Today is the Anniversary of:

_____

_____

Prayer: *Lord, may we never cease to give thanks that You are God and came to us as the divine embodiment of Your great love for Your people.*

JUNE 28th

St. Irenaeus, Martyr

Defender of the faith in the 2nd century, Saint Irenaeus reminds us how precious is the gift of faith.

Today is the Birthday of:

Today is the Anniversary of:

Prayer: *Loving God, please help me to spend time studying the teachings of theologians—past and present.*

JUNE 29th

Sts. Peter and Paul

Saint Peter, the original "fisher of men," and the indefatigable St. Paul teach us that God chooses the most ordinary of people to serve His Church.

Today is the Birthday of:

Today is the Anniversary of:

Prayer: *Jesus, help me to realize that my flaws are not an impediment to Your love and guidance.*

JUNE 30th

St. Bertrand

Saint Bertrand shows us the necessity of cultivating and nurturing people just as we might cultivate a garden.

Today is the Birthday of:

Today is the Anniversary of:

Prayer: *Nurturing God, give me the empathy and compassion to "grow" people toward You and toward loving one another.*

As the Father has loved me, so I have loved you.

John 15:9

JULY 1st

St. Aaron

By proclaiming God to pharaoh, Saint Aaron, brother of Moses, inspires us to speak fearlessly of God's majesty.

Today is the Birthday of:

Today is the Anniversary of:

Prayer: *Father, help me to emulate Moses, Aaron, and their sister Miriam, ancestors of my faith.*

JULY 2nd

St. Bernardino Realino

We strive to follow Saint Bernardino's example of unsurpassing kindness to all and peace-making among those who were divided.

Today is the Birthday of:

Today is the Anniversary of:

Prayer: *Jesus, help me to put aside my judgments so I can show kindness to all I meet and demonstrate the promise of peace.*

JULY 3rd

St. Thomas, Apostle

Saint Thomas, whose skepticism was rewarded with proof of Jesus' resurrection, helps us face our doubts.

Today is the Birthday of:

Today is the Anniversary of:

Prayer: *Lord, You comforted and reassured Thomas; I pray that You do the same with me when I am confused and assailed by doubts.*

JULY 4th

St. Elizabeth of Portugal

From Saint Elizabeth we learn that gentleness and patience are the weapons with which true Christian warriors win souls.

Today is the Birthday of:

Today is the Anniversary of:

Prayer: *Father, help me to be a peacemaker at home, at work, and wherever there is discord.*

JULY 5th

St. Anthony Zaccaria

Saint Anthony's work as both physician and priest teaches us that God wants us to heal souls as well as bodies.

Today is the Birthday of:

Today is the Anniversary of:

Prayer: *Healing God, grant that I attend to both body and soul, knowing that the two are intricately connected.*

JULY 6th

St. Maria Goretti, Martyr

Saint Maria, Patroness of Youth, demonstrates how important it is for us to both forgive and to pray for others to forgive.

Today is the Birthday of:

Today is the Anniversary of:

Prayer: *Father, help me to be the first to forgive and by my example help others to forgive from their hearts.*

JULY 7th

Bl. Ralph Milner and Roger Dickenson, Martyrs

Blessed Ralph and Blessed Roger show us how lay people and clergy can be instrumental in defending and proclaiming faith.

Today is the Birthday of:

Today is the Anniversary of:

Prayer: *God, give me the courage and insight to avoid hypocrisy in all its forms, especially in religion.*

JULY 8th

Sts. Prisca and Aquila

Married saints Prisca and Aquila remind us of the need to have "church" and thus, God's presence, within our homes.

Today is the Birthday of:

_____

_____

_____

Today is the Anniversary of:

_____

_____

Prayer: *Father, let me be conscious every day of Your presence in my home and making it a place where Your presence shines.*

JULY 9th

St. Augustine Zhao Rong and Companions, Martyrs

Saint Augustine Zhao Rong and over 100 Chinese Christians were marked by joy showing that fidelity to Jesus frees us.

Today is the Birthday of:

_____

_____

_____

Today is the Anniversary of:

_____

_____

Prayer: *I give all thanks to You, Jesus, for sending Your Spirit into the hearts and minds of people all over the world.*

JULY 10th

St. Canute, Martyr

Through Saint Canute's life, we see the damaging power of family jealousy and work to avoid it in our families.

Today is the Birthday of:

Today is the Anniversary of:

Prayer: *Father God, oversee my family and all who are close to me so that envy and anger never separate us.*

JULY 11th

St. Benedict

Patron of Poison Victims, Saint Benedict demonstrates that faith in God is an antidote to the poison of sin.

Today is the Birthday of:

Today is the Anniversary of:

Prayer: *Forgiving God, grant me the grace to turn away from sin with sincere remorse and repentance.*

JULY 12th

St. John Gualbert

By freeing his enemy, Saint John teaches us that we should never seek revenge and always accept God as judge.

Today is the Birthday of:

_____

_____

_____

Today is the Anniversary of:

_____

_____

Prayer: *Merciful God, remind me that only You can properly judge and turn me from the sin of revenge.*

JULY 13th

St. Henry II

Emperor and Patron of the Disadvantaged, Saint Henry shows that the best leaders put the needs of those they serve first.

Today is the Birthday of:

Today is the Anniversary of:

Prayer: *Watchful God, give me the insight to support those leaders who treat the poor and disenfranchised with respect and care.*

JULY 14th

St. Francis Solano

Called the apostle of South America for his evangelizing power, Saint Francis Solano embodied Jesus' words: "Blessed are the peacemakers."

Today is the Birthday of:

Today is the Anniversary of:

Prayer: *Jesus, please help me to promote peace and to practice all the beatitudes.*

JULY 15th

St. Bonaventure

Saint Bonaventure's reluctance to accept unwanted titles reminds us that we must sometimes accept greater responsibilities.

Today is the Birthday of:

Today is the Anniversary of:

Prayer: *Beloved Father, give me the courage to humbly accept those responsibilities which will enrich Your Kingdom.*

JULY 16th

St. Mary-Magdalene Postel

In her work to educate girls, Saint Mary-Magdalen Postel illustrates the importance of teaching the young about our faith.

Today is the Birthday of:

Today is the Anniversary of:

Prayer: *Lord, I thank You for all the teachers, especially the religious sisters, who educate, strengthen, and encourage us.*

JULY 17th

The Blessed Martyrs of Compiègne

These sixteen holy women proved that no revolution, or change in government should alter our words and acts of faith.

Today is the Birthday of:

_____

_____

_____

Today is the Anniversary of:

_____

_____

Prayer: *Father, I pray that I confront any challenges to my faith with dignity, faith, and praise for You.*

JULY 18th

St. Camillus de Lellis

Patron of Hospitals, Saint Camillus shows us that we must reach out to the sick in hospitals and health care facilities.

Today is the Birthday of:

Today is the Anniversary of:

Prayer: *Lord, give me the strength and humility to be a channel of Your healing.*

JULY 19th

St. Macrina the Younger

Saint Macrina shows us that we may be strengthened and edified through the word of God in the Psalms and the Book of Wisdom.

Today is the Birthday of:

Today is the Anniversary of:

Prayer: *Father, give me the discernment to embrace Your holy word in the scriptures and other sacred writings.*

JULY 20th

St. Apollinaris, Martyr

The cures attributed to Saint Apollinaris remind us of how God touches us lovingly through those He chooses.

Today is the Birthday of:

Today is the Anniversary of:

Prayer: *Jesus, let me be a healer of hearts and souls as I seek to do Your work today.*

JULY 21st

St. Lawrence of Brindisi

Saint Lawrence's mastery of many languages demonstrates that no barriers exist for those who speak of God's majestic presence.

Today is the Birthday of:

Today is the Anniversary of:

Prayer: *Lord of all tongues, may Your spirit open my mouth to proclaim Your word to all hearers.*

JULY 22nd

St. Mary Magdalene

The first to encounter the risen Jesus, Saint Mary Magdalene embodies the wondrous joy of experiencing the resurrection.

Today is the Birthday of:

Today is the Anniversary of:

Prayer: *Jesus, fill me with the joy that illumined Mary Magdalene's life: the knowledge of You, risen! Alleluia!*

JULY 23rd

St. John Cassian

Saint Cassian's loyalty to his teacher, Saint John Chrysostom, inspires us to support each other in our faith and good works.

☙ ☙ ☙

Today is the Birthday of:

Today is the Anniversary of:

Prayer: *Father, thank You for the blessing of being one part among many of the Body of Christ.*

JULY 24th

St. Sharbel Makhlouf

Born in Lebanon, Saint Sharbel Makhlouf reminds us to pray for all Christians in the troubled, divided Middle East.

Today is the Birthday of:

_____

_____

_____

Today is the Anniversary of:

_____

_____

Prayer: *Jesus, send Your peace upon the people of the Middle East; help them to live and work together.*

JULY 25th

St. James, Apostle

Apostle and Patron of Laborers Saint James reminds us it is not enough to profess faith; we must do the work of faith.

Today is the Birthday of:

Today is the Anniversary of:

Prayer: *Father, let my hands and body be as strong in expressing faith as my lips and tongue.*

JULY 26th

Bl. Titus Brandsma, Martyr

Blessed Titus' resistance of the Nazis earned him martyrdom and our admiration for his courage, selflessness, and faith.

Today is the Birthday of:

Today is the Anniversary of:

Prayer: *Lord, I pray for all martyrs of the 20th century who present models for us all in resisting great evil.*

JULY 27th

St. Pantaleon, Martyr

Patron of Physicians, Saint Pantaleon illustrates that all Christians should strive to reveal God through their work.

Today is the Birthday of:

Today is the Anniversary of:

Prayer: *Father of all, thank You for the doctors, nurses, and health care professionals You have sent to help us.*

JULY 28th

St. Samson

Saint Samson's great humility in refusing all honors inspires us to work for God and not our own advancement.

Today is the Birthday of:

Today is the Anniversary of:

Prayer: *Jesus, cleanse me of all tendencies to pride and arrogance, and teach me gentle humility.*

JULY 29th

St. Martha

By both serving Jesus and proclaiming her faith in Him, Saint Martha illustrates the two aspects of faith we strive for.

Today is the Birthday of:

Today is the Anniversary of:

Prayer: *Lord, let me be of service to You both in manual work and in how I speak of You to others.*

JULY 30th

St. Leopold Mandic

Like July's flower, the larkspur, Saint Leopold represented great open-heartedness as he heard confessions and encouraged conversion.

Today is the Birthday of:

_____

_____

_____

Today is the Anniversary of:

_____

_____

Prayer: *God, help me to receive all who come to me for help or advice, with an open and generous spirit.*

JULY 31st

St. Ignatius of Loyola

Patron of Retreats, Saint Ignatius founded the Jesuits, giving us a religious order that has brilliantly defended our faith.

Today is the Birthday of:

Today is the Anniversary of:

Prayer: *Father, I thank You for the preaching and teaching of all religious sisters, brothers, and priests.*

That friendship of which Jesus is the link is strong and everlasting.

St. Francis de Sales

AUGUST 1st

*The Seven Holy Macabees
and St. Eleazar, Martyrs*

We admire these holy men who were martyred for refusing to break the laws of God revealed to them by Moses.

Today is the Birthday of:

_____

_____

_____

Today is the Anniversary of:

_____

_____

Prayer: *Creator God, teach me to respect all men and women who suffer in order to stay loyal to You.*

AUGUST 2nd

St. Peter Julian Eymard

Saint Peter Julian's devotion to the Holy Eucharist led him to bring others to the sacrament, a dedication we should emulate.

Today is the Birthday of:

Today is the Anniversary of:

Prayer: *Jesus, let me never cease praising You in the sacrament of the Holy Eucharist.*

AUGUST 3rd

Bl. Augustine Gazotich

Blessed Augustine shows the need for renewal in faith, motivating us to seek fresh ways to be closer to God.

Today is the Birthday of:

Today is the Anniversary of:

Prayer: *Father, lead me to seek out new ways to express my dedication to You.*

AUGUST 4th

St. Ia, Martyr

Saint Ia's perseverance in faith invites us to re-commit ourselves daily to God.

※ ※ ※

Today is the Birthday of:

Today is the Anniversary of:

Prayer: *God, imbue me with the strength of a martyr and spare me such a test.*

AUGUST 5th

St. Oswald of Northumbria

Saint Oswald reminds us that we need to gather and share with other Christians to "spread the faith."

Today is the Birthday of:

_____

_____

_____

Today is the Anniversary of:

_____

_____

Prayer: *Lord, give me the discernment to recognize those You send to increase my faith.*

AUGUST 6th

The Transfiguration

Through His Transfiguration, Jesus demonstrated that He was God's chosen, the One known even by Moses and Elijah.

Today is the Birthday of:

_____

_____

Today is the Anniversary of:

_____

_____

Prayer: *Transfigured Jesus, I thank You for giving us all that we need to recognize You as God's own Son.*

AUGUST 7th

St. Cajetan

Saint Cajetan teaches us that we should all seek to live the simple, faithful, prayerful, helpful life of apostles.

Today is the Birthday of:

Today is the Anniversary of:

Prayer: *Holy Spirit, give me the courage and selflessness to live as a disciple of Christ.*

AUGUST 8th

St. Dominic

Founder of the Order of Preachers, we pray the Rosary because of Dominic's example.

Today is the Birthday of:

Today is the Anniversary of:

Prayer: *God of judgment, thank You for those religious men and women who defy the world and its values in order to stay close to You.*

AUGUST 9th

St. Teresa Benedicta of the Cross (Edith Stein), Martyr

Convert, philosopher, teacher and martyr, Saint Teresa Benedicta exemplifies how God moves through a single devoted life.

Today is the Birthday of:

Today is the Anniversary of:

Prayer: *Father, I thank You for converts like Saint Teresa Benedicta, who take my breath away with their courage, and devotion to You.*

AUGUST 10th

St. Lawrence, Martyr

Patron of the Poor, Saint Lawrence courted martyrdom in his commitment to caring for the poor as Jesus instructed us.

Today is the Birthday of:

_____

_____

Today is the Anniversary of:

_____

_____

Prayer: *Kind Jesus, may I treasure the poor as You did, and help them always.*

AUGUST 11th

St. Clare

Friend of St. Francis, founder of the Poor Clares, we learn through St. Clare selfless dedication to Christ.

Today is the Birthday of:

Today is the Anniversary of:

Prayer: *Eucharistic God, strengthen our faith by devotion to the Blessed Sacrament.*

AUGUST 12th

St. Euplius, Martyr

Saint Euplius died rather than reject the Gospels, reminding us of how easily we may access God's word today.

Today is the Birthday of:

_____

_____

_____

Today is the Anniversary of:

_____

_____

Prayer: *God of all knowledge, teach me to seek Your wisdom in the Gospels in all situations.*

AUGUST 13th

∽∽

St. John Berchmans

Patron of Altar Servers, Saint John motivates us to encourage our young people to serve God from their earliest days.

Today is the Birthday of:

Today is the Anniversary of:

Prayer: *Father of all, I pray that You keep Your Church strong through the commitment of its youth.*

AUGUST 14th

St. Maximilian Mary Kolbe, Martyr

In giving his life for another in Auschwitz, Saint Maximilian reminds us that Jesus gave His life for every person.

Today is the Birthday of:

_____

_____

_____

Today is the Anniversary of:

_____

_____

Prayer: *Comforter of the Afflicted, help me to free those who are imprisoned in heart, mind and soul.*

AUGUST 15th

*St. Tarcisius,
Martyr of the Holy Eucharist*

Patron of First Communicants, Saint Tarcisius gave his life for the Eucharist, reminding us of the primacy of this Sacrament.

Today is the Birthday of:

_____

_____

_____

Today is the Anniversary of:

_____

_____

Prayer: *Jesus, every time I receive the Holy Eucharist may it be with the same awe and gratitude that I felt at my first Holy Communion.*

AUGUST 16th

St. Stephen

As a king, saint, and devoted servant of Mary, Stephen demonstrates that those who follow God are worthy of being followed by us.

Today is the Birthday of:

Today is the Anniversary of:

Prayer: *Father, I pray that You provide leaders for Your world who do Your will and put You above all else.*

AUGUST 17th

St. Joan Delanoue

Saint Joan Delanoue's selfless work on behalf of orphans reminds us of scripture's frequent direction to care for orphans.

Today is the Birthday of:

Today is the Anniversary of:

Prayer: *Loving Father, help me to reach out to those who have no parents, especially those who do not yet know You as the ultimate Parent.*

AUGUST 18th

St. Jane Frances de Chantal

Like August's flower, the poppy, Saint Jane Frances' life represents a commitment to marriage, family, and love of God.

Today is the Birthday of:

Today is the Anniversary of:

Prayer: *Beloved God, move me to embrace the way You select for me to serve You.*

AUGUST 19th

St. John Eudes

Saint John Eudes reveals that we need not travel outside our own borders to be missionaries if we follow God.

❧ ❧ ❧

Today is the Birthday of:

Today is the Anniversary of:

Prayer: *Father, help me to reveal You to those I meet wherever I am, especially in "my own backyard."*

AUGUST 20th

St. Mary de Matthias

Saint Mary promoted education in the face of opposition, reminding us of the importance of nurturing our children.

Today is the Birthday of:

_____

_____

_____

Today is the Anniversary of:

_____

_____

Prayer: *Teaching Lord, give me the strength to work for excellent schools in the knowledge that our children are our future.*

AUGUST 21st

St. Pius X

Pope and Saint, Pius X taught us to reject wealth, even that of the Church, in favor of humility and simplicity.

Today is the Birthday of:

Today is the Anniversary of:

Prayer: *All-renewing God, help me to focus on the things of God; let me never be a slave to money.*

AUGUST 22nd

St. Philip Benizi

By rejecting the prospect of being chosen pope, Saint Philip Benizi teaches us the importance of humble service.

Today is the Birthday of:

_____

_____

_____

Today is the Anniversary of:

_____

_____

Prayer: *Father, teach me not to love honors and recognition as much as serving and following You.*

AUGUST 23rd

St. Rose of Lima

Known as the originator of social service in Peru, Saint Rose demonstrates that to love Jesus we must help others.

Today is the Birthday of:

Today is the Anniversary of:

Prayer: *Jesus, move me to assist those in the world who are poor, alone, and without resources.*

AUGUST 24th

St. Bartholomew, Apostle

Chosen by Jesus, Saint Bartholomew inspires us by giving his life to evangelize in the most difficult regions of the world.

Today is the Birthday of:

Today is the Anniversary of:

Prayer: *Jesus, give me the courage of those who walked with You as I try to follow in their footsteps.*

AUGUST 25th

St. Genesius, Martyr

Patron of Actors and Musicians, Saint Genesius reminds us that faith can be gloriously expressed when art is inspired by God.

Today is the Birthday of:

Today is the Anniversary of:

Prayer: *God of diversity, teach me to seek Your Presence in every facet of life and art.*

AUGUST 26th

St. Teresa of Jesus Ibars

Saint Teresa of Jesus Ibars, founder of the Little Sisters of the Poor, teaches us to overcome rejection when seeking God's plan.

Today is the Birthday of:

Today is the Anniversary of:

Prayer: *Thank You, dear Jesus, for loving me.*

AUGUST 27th

St. Monica

Patroness of Mothers and Widows, Saint Monica's prayers for her son Augustine's conversion, inspire us to never abandon hope.

❦   ❦   ❦

Today is the Birthday of:

Today is the Anniversary of:

Prayer: *Divine Parent, help me to be someone who inspires my parents, children, and family to greater faith.*

AUGUST 28th

St. Moses the Black, Martyr

Like his namesake, Saint Moses' journey began with crime and ended in serving God, revealing the power of conversion.

Today is the Birthday of:

Today is the Anniversary of:

Prayer: *God, let me be a help and never an impediment to those who might convert their lives to You.*

AUGUST 29th

St. Sabina, Martyr

By allowing her slave to convert her, Saint Sabina teaches us to never dismiss someone God might have sent us.

Today is the Birthday of:

_____

_____

_____

Today is the Anniversary of:

_____

_____

Prayer: *Father, help me to look for Your messengers and Your messages in places where I may not expect them to be.*

AUGUST 30th

St. Fiacre

Patron of Gardeners, Saint Fiacre demonstrates that the simple and generous act of feeding people can win souls.

Today is the Birthday of:

Today is the Anniversary of:

Prayer: *Jesus, the next time I am shopping, remind me to fill a bag for a local soup kitchen, shelter, or neighborhood family.*

AUGUST 31st

~~~

Sts. Joseph of Arimathea and Nicodemus

Blessed with the keeping of Jesus' body, Saints Joseph of Arimathea and Nicodemus teach us to express reverence for the human body.

༺ ༺ ༺

Today is the Birthday of:

_____

_____

_____

Today is the Anniversary of:

_____

_____

Prayer: *Jesus, Whose death I grieve, I give thanks for those who attend to the dead and to their loved ones.*

Love

one

another.

John 15:17

SEPTEMBER 1st

St. Giles

Patron of the Crippled, Saint Giles reveals that the wholeness of our bodies is not as important as the strength of our souls.

Today is the Birthday of:

_____

_____

_____

Today is the Anniversary of:

_____

_____

Prayer: *Lord, help me to remember that even when my body lets me down, I can work to keep my soul from letting You—and me—down.*

SEPTEMBER 2nd

Bl. Solomon Le Clerq, Martyr

Blessed Solomon shows us that sainthood does not require exceptional piety, just deep devotion to God, and prayer.

Today is the Birthday of:

Today is the Anniversary of:

Prayer: *Father, help me to remember that what I lack in skills and talents can never keep me from You.*

SEPTEMBER 3rd

St. Gregory the Great

Patron of Musicians and Teachers, Pope St. Gregory emphasized the Liturgy of the Mass and the Divine Office.

Today is the Birthday of:

Today is the Anniversary of:

Prayer: *Holy God, may I become a more integral part of my parish community through the prayer of the Church.*

SEPTEMBER 4th

St. Moses, Prophet and Lawgiver

By leading the Israelites out of slavery to God's promised land, Moses gives us our history.

Today is the Birthday of:

Today is the Anniversary of:

Prayer: *God, help me to appreciate my firm foundation of faith from Moses and the later prophets.*

SEPTEMBER 5th

Bl. Teresa of Calcutta

We learn perseverance from Bl. Teresa's commitment to God's poor despite her struggles of faith.

Today is the Birthday of:

Today is the Anniversary of:

Prayer: *Father, like Blessed Teresa let me never put anything between me and serving You.*

SEPTEMBER 6th

St. Zechariah, Prophet

Saint Zechariah's words that show God's plan for history give us great hope.

Today is the Birthday of:

_____

_____

Today is the Anniversary of:

_____

_____

Prayer: *Savior Lord, let us never cease praising and thanking You for Your goodness and love.*

SEPTEMBER 7th

St. Regina, Martyr

Saint Regina's faith journey with her Christian nurse reveals how we can change others' lives by our example.

Today is the Birthday of:

Today is the Anniversary of:

Prayer: *Jesus, bring me to those who I can help and who help me by modeling Christianity.*

SEPTEMBER 8th

The Nativity of Mary

We are comforted that Mary, though born without sin, suffered the same human difficulties from birth to death that we suffer.

Today is the Birthday of:

Today is the Anniversary of:

Prayer: *Father, You chose Mary to bear Your Son and our Savior; teach me to turn to her as an example of perfect obedience.*

SEPTEMBER 9th

St. Peter Claver

Patron of the Missions to Black people, Saint Peter Claver teaches us to reveal Christ by materially aiding all who are enslaved.

Today is the Birthday of:

Today is the Anniversary of:

Prayer: *Jesus, help me to embrace all people, regardless of their skin color, language, religion, or social status.*

SEPTEMBER 10th

St. Nicholas of Tolentine

As the Patron of Mariners, Saint Nicholas reminds us how all travelers who sincerely seek God's protection, will have it.

Today is the Birthday of:

Today is the Anniversary of:

Prayer: *Watchful God, I thank You for providing me with refuge whenever I need it; stay close to me, Lord!*

SEPTEMBER 11th

St. John Gabriel Perboyre, Martyr

Saint John Gabriel helped abandoned children in China, reminding us that Christian actions speak louder than words.

Today is the Birthday of:

Today is the Anniversary of:

Prayer: *Lord, lead me to help children and youth so that the next generation may be Yours.*

SEPTEMBER 12th

St. Guy of Anderlecht

Miracles associated with Saint Guy teach us that God's most humble servants are also often His most gifted servants.

Today is the Birthday of:

Today is the Anniversary of:

Prayer: *Father, thank You for men and women who remind me to be humble in all that I do and say.*

SEPTEMBER 13th

༄༅

St. John Chrysostom

Patron of Sacred Orators, Saint John Chrysostom demonstrates how the desire to speak always of Christ makes us eloquent.

Today is the Birthday of:

Today is the Anniversary of:

Prayer: *Teaching Jesus, give me the courage to speak of Your ways to everyone who has ears to hear.*

SEPTEMBER 14th

Exaltation of the Holy Cross

The Exaltation of the Holy Cross reveals Jesus' priceless sacrifice in allowing Himself to die on the cross for us.

Today is the Birthday of:

Today is the Anniversary of:

Prayer: *Lord, let me proudly display the cross so that I never forget what You did for me.*

SEPTEMBER 15th

∽∽

St. Catherine of Genoa

Saint Catherine's suffering and labor among the sick demonstrate that mystics can also be practical workers for God.

Today is the Birthday of:

Today is the Anniversary of:

Prayer: *Loving God, remind me of my two-fold call: to pray and to serve.*

SEPTEMBER 16th

St. Edith of Wilton

Like September's flower, the morning glory, symbolizing devotion, Saint Edith models how devotion to God surpasses worldly attention.

Today is the Birthday of:

Today is the Anniversary of:

Prayer: *Father, help me to follow Your voice when the world demands my attention.*

SEPTEMBER 17th

St. Robert Bellarmine

Patron of Canonists, Saint Robert's commitment to Christian learning is what we strive for in our quest to follow God.

Today is the Birthday of:

_____

_____

_____

Today is the Anniversary of:

_____

_____

Prayer: *Beloved God, help me to seek You through study, meditation, and through those You send to me.*

SEPTEMBER 18th

St. Joseph of Cupertino

We take delight in Saint Joseph, Patron of Aviators, who, in his great love for God, often rose into the air.

Today is the Birthday of:

Today is the Anniversary of:

Prayer: *Father, raise me up where I belong and where others will see the joy You bring to those who love You.*

SEPTEMBER 19th

St. Emily De Rodat

Saint Emily shows us how one simple service to God can expand into a multitude of good.

Today is the Birthday of:

_____

_____

_____

Today is the Anniversary of:

_____

_____

Prayer: *Jesus, when I am feeling low, encourage me to do just the one thing, and then the next, and the next.*

SEPTEMBER 20th

St. Eustace, Martyr

Saint Eustace who won and lost great wealth and victories, is proof that only devotion to God is of value.

Today is the Birthday of:

Today is the Anniversary of:

Prayer: *Beloved God, whether life lifts me high or brings me low, help me to keep my attention focused on You.*

SEPTEMBER 21st

St. Matthew, Apostle and Evangelist

Matthew who wrote his Gospel for a Jewish Christian community expresses God's all-embracing love.

Today is the Birthday of:

Today is the Anniversary of:

Prayer: *God of all, I beg You to draw me to You and to help me to respond with Matthew's fervor.*

SEPTEMBER 22nd

St. Emmerammus

Saint Emmerammus shows us that if we are to be missionaries for Jesus, we must be ready to pay a price.

Today is the Birthday of:

Today is the Anniversary of:

Prayer: *Lord, when following You leads me to a place where I am in danger, please encourage and protect me.*

SEPTEMBER 23rd

St. Pio of Pietrelcina

Padre Pio's life and Stigmata inspire us to follow Christ closely and to transform suffering.

Today is the Birthday of:

_____

_____

Today is the Anniversary of:

_____

_____

Prayer: *Healing Jesus, may the wounds and life of Padre Pio remind me of Your presence in every person.*

SEPTEMBER 24th

St. Pacific of San Severino

Saint Pacific exemplifies how God can transform illnesses into opportunities for prayer and discipleship.

Today is the Birthday of:

Today is the Anniversary of:

Prayer: *Father, show me how to grow closer to You through all the obstacles in my life.*

SEPTEMBER 25th

St. Cleophas, Disciple of Christ

Saint Cleophas' meeting with the risen Lord on the way to Emmaus teaches us how God turns despair into joyful hope.

Today is the Birthday of:

Today is the Anniversary of:

Prayer: *Risen Jesus, reveal Yourself to me when I am dejected and despairing, so that I, too, may dance.*

SEPTEMBER 26th

St. Theresa Couderc

Founder of the Cenacle Sisters, St. Theresa's followers focus on retreats for lay people.

Today is the Birthday of:

Today is the Anniversary of:

Prayer: *Peaceful God, help me to heed Your invitation to come apart and rest with You.*

SEPTEMBER 27th

St. Vincent De Paul

Saint Vincent De Paul, Apostle of Charity, epitomizes serving those in need, as is evident in many cities today.

Today is the Birthday of:

Today is the Anniversary of:

Prayer: *Jesus, help me to help those in need through organizations inspired by charitable men and women.*

SEPTEMBER 28th

St. Wenceslaus, Martyr

Saint Wenceslaus teaches us to embrace and proclaim Christianity even when our family members reject Your love.

Today is the Birthday of:

Today is the Anniversary of:

Prayer: *King of Kings, Lord of Lords, may I proclaim Your name above all names.*

SEPTEMBER 29th

Sts. Michael, Gabriel, Raphael, Archangels

These three Angels remind us that we are never far from God's protection and healing.

Today is the Birthday of:

Today is the Anniversary of:

Prayer: *God of wisdom and strength, may Your Angels who minister to You in heaven, defend us here on earth.*

SEPTEMBER 30th

St. Jerome

Patron of Librarians, Saint Jerome teaches us gratitude for those whose learning benefits and advances all of us.

Today is the Birthday of:

Today is the Anniversary of:

Prayer: *Lord, lead me to the teachers and the writings that will strengthen my faith.*

Of all that are dear to you, let Jesus be your special friend.

Bk. 2, 8.
Imitation of Christ

OCTOBER 1st

St. Therese of the Child Jesus

Saint Therese, also called the Little Flower, reminds us that complete love of God is the only proper foundation for life.

Today is the Birthday of:

Today is the Anniversary of:

Prayer: *Father, help me to know that all sacred texts and inspired sermons lead to one conclusion: You are love.*

OCTOBER 2nd

～～～

The Guardian Angels

Protectors and defenders of all people, nations and churches, Guardian Angels offer continuous praise to God.

❦ ❦ ❦

Today is the Birthday of:

_____

_____

_____

Today is the Anniversary of:

_____

_____

Prayer: *Watchful God, may we always be under the protection of Your Angels and one day enjoy their company in heaven.*

OCTOBER 3rd

St. Hesychius

Saint Hesychius illustrates how important it is to find and keep in our lives those who lead us to God.

Today is the Birthday of:

Today is the Anniversary of:

Prayer: *God, give me the humility and the tenacity to stay close to those who will bring me closer to You.*

OCTOBER 4th

St. Francis of Assisi

Patron of Ecologists, Saint Francis reminds us to see God in all creation and to respect His gifts of the earth.

Today is the Birthday of:

Today is the Anniversary of:

Prayer: *Creator God, I rejoice in all creation; help me to be a good and grateful steward.*

OCTOBER 5th

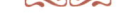

St. Faustina Kowalska

Saint Faustina's life and diary reveal how utterly we must trust in Jesus' Divine Mercy in our lives and our world.

Today is the Birthday of:

Today is the Anniversary of:

Prayer: *Kind Jesus, remind me that no one who prays for forgiveness is outside of Your Divine Mercy.*

OCTOBER 6th

Bl. Isidore of Saint Joseph

Blessed Isidore demonstrates to us the value of nurturing Christian community in church, society, and all we do.

Today is the Birthday of:

Today is the Anniversary of:

Prayer: *Lord, help me to reach out to create the proactive bonds of community with those in my world.*

OCTOBER 7th

St. Mark

An early pope, Saint Mark shows that God's plan for His Church and world is often too wonderful to comprehend.

Today is the Birthday of:

Today is the Anniversary of:

Prayer: *Father, help me to remember that my job is not to understand, but to obey and trust in Your providence.*

OCTOBER 8th

St. Reparata, Martyr

Martyred for her faith while still a child, Saint Reparata reminds us of what many suffered for their love of God.

Today is the Birthday of:

_____

_____

_____

Today is the Anniversary of:

_____

_____

Prayer: *Almighty God, when I lose faith because of the trials of life, let me take courage in Your faithfulness.*

OCTOBER 9th

St. Abraham

Father of All Believers, Saint Abraham reveals how close God comes to, and how much He demands from, those He chooses.

Today is the Birthday of:

Today is the Anniversary of:

Prayer: *God of Abraham, I rejoice in Your friendship with the men and women who dedicate their lives to You.*

OCTOBER 10th

~~~

St. Paulinus of York

Saint Paulinus illustrates that winning converts requires us to have great patience and sometimes to make great sacrifices.

~~~ ~~~ ~~~

Today is the Birthday of:

_____

_____

_____

Today is the Anniversary of:

_____

_____

Prayer: *Lord, let me never grow weary of revealing Your glory to those who take a long time to believe.*

OCTOBER 11th

St. Mary Soledad

We emulate Saint Mary who, faced with her own illness, fashioned a life dedicated to helping the poor and ill.

Today is the Birthday of:

Today is the Anniversary of:

Prayer: *Father, show me the way to turn my illnesses into positive actions through the Holy Spirit.*

OCTOBER 12th

Sts. Cyprian and Felix, Martyrs

Separated by decades in age, Saints Cyprian and Felix remind us that age is meaningless in our commitment to God.

Today is the Birthday of:

Today is the Anniversary of:

Prayer: *Loving Parent, help me to imitate those who sacrifice their comfort for others.*

OCTOBER 13th

St. Gerald of Aurillac

Saint Gerald demonstrates that those who cannot see and do not esteem the things of the world, may better experience God.

Today is the Birthday of:

Today is the Anniversary of:

Prayer: *Lord, when I am blinded by the glitter of the world, lead me to You through prayer and meditation.*

OCTOBER 14th

St. Callistus I, Martyr

From slave to pope, Saint Callistus' renowned compassion and forgiveness are qualities we should strive for.

Today is the Birthday of:

_____

_____

_____

Today is the Anniversary of:

_____

_____

Prayer: *Compassionate Father, help me to learn from my own misfortunes to shower mercy on others.*

OCTOBER 15th

St. Teresa of Avila

Recognized for her wisdom and writing, Saint Teresa shows us that we must use our God-given talents to strengthen faith.

Today is the Birthday of:

_____

_____

_____

Today is the Anniversary of:

_____

_____

Prayer: *Generous God, thank You for the inspiration of sacred writings which bolster my faith and hope.*

OCTOBER 16th

St. Gerard Majella

Known for his great piety and wisdom, St. Gerard is invoked as a Patron of expectant mothers.

Today is the Birthday of:

Today is the Anniversary of:

Prayer: *Father, help me to be "carried away" by and for You, to faithfully follow Your plan.*

OCTOBER 17th

St. Ignatius of Antioch, Martyr

Saint Ignatius' enthusiasm and sacrifice illustrate how completely Jesus changed His world, and ours.

Today is the Birthday of:

Today is the Anniversary of:

Prayer: *Jesus, instill in me the same devotion and enthusiasm that illuminated the lives of the early Christians.*

OCTOBER 18th

St. Luke

Author of the third Gospel and Patron of Doctors, Saint Luke inspires us to fully serve God.

Today is the Birthday of:

Today is the Anniversary of:

Prayer: *Jesus, teach me never to limit myself as I seek to reveal You through my words and work.*

OCTOBER 19th

Sts. Isaac Jogues, John de Brebeuf and Companions, Martyrs

These North American martyrs instill in us single-minded devotion to God.

Today is the Birthday of:

_____

_____

_____

Today is the Anniversary of:

_____

_____

Prayer: *Welcoming God, let me bring peace to those who do not know Your justice and mercy.*

OCTOBER 20th

St. Paul of the Cross

Saint Paul reminds us that we can be both spiritually attracted to the Lord and His most pragmatic laborers.

ଦୃତ୍ତ   ଦୃତ୍ତ   ଦୃତ୍ତ

Today is the Birthday of:

Today is the Anniversary of:

Prayer: *Perfect God, help me to find the right balance between contemplation and action.*

OCTOBER 21st

St. Celine

Like St. Elizabeth, John's mother, this Saint gave birth to St. Remigius at an advanced age.

Today is the Birthday of:

Today is the Anniversary of:

Prayer: *Father, when I am deterred by signs of aging, remind me of Your power working through me.*

OCTOBER 22nd

St. Donatus

Scholar and soldier, Saint Donatus shows us that when God leads us, our supposed destination might not be the point of the journey.

Today is the Birthday of:

Today is the Anniversary of:

Prayer: *Lord, make me willing to go where You lead me, even if it turns out to be a surprise!*

OCTOBER 23rd

St. John of Capistrano

Saint John, a lawyer and Patron of Jurists, teaches the importance of employing wisdom and humility in our decisions.

Today is the Birthday of:

Today is the Anniversary of:

Prayer: *Father, help me to always seek Your direction and guidance to make important decisions.*

OCTOBER 24th

St. Martin of Vertou

Failing as a preacher, Saint Martin's success in attracting believers by his simple goodness reminds us to persevere.

Today is the Birthday of:

Today is the Anniversary of:

Prayer: *Creator God, may my strengths and my weaknesses keep me on Your path.*

OCTOBER 25th

Sts. Crispin and Crispinian, Martyrs

Shoemakers who served the poor for free, Saints Crispin and Crispinian teach us there are many ways to be missionaries.

Today is the Birthday of:

Today is the Anniversary of:

Prayer: *Lord, show me the ways I may use my daily work to reveal Your loving presence to all people.*

OCTOBER 26th

St. Rusticus

Saint Rusticus shows us that when we become overwhelmed, God will send the strength to continue the work He's given us.

Today is the Birthday of:

_____

_____

_____

Today is the Anniversary of:

_____

_____

Prayer: *Father, when I am too weak to carry my burdens, remind me that You are near.*

OCTOBER 27th

St. Namatius

By sponsoring a "Bible of the Poor" of paintings telling Bible stories, Saint Namatius shows how our creativity can serve God.

Today is the Birthday of:

Today is the Anniversary of:

Prayer: *Beloved Creator, show me how to use my imagination and my creativity to better serve You.*

OCTOBER 28th

St. Jude

Saint Jude, Apostle of Jesus and Patron of Desperate Cases, reminds us that God will never abandon us.

Today is the Birthday of:

Today is the Anniversary of:

Prayer: *Jesus, I thank You for men and women like Saint Jude who give me hope through the trials I face.*

OCTOBER 29th

St. Narcissus

Saint Narcissus demonstrates that God will protect and guide us when our enemies place obstacles before us.

Today is the Birthday of:

Today is the Anniversary of:

Prayer: *Loving Father, gather me into Your arms and keep me safe from those who would hurt me.*

OCTOBER 30th

St. Marcellus the Centurion, Martyr

We admire Saint Marcellus for understanding that when we make God our priority, we can also serve our country.

Today is the Birthday of:

Today is the Anniversary of:

Prayer: *God of Light, when I am confused about how to serve You and my community, show me Your way.*

OCTOBER 31st

St. Wolfgang

Like October's flower, the marigold, which symbolizes excellence, Saint Wolfgang demonstrates excellence in his work for God.

Today is the Birthday of:

Today is the Anniversary of:

Prayer: *Beloved Lord, lead me to strive humbly for excellence in all that I undertake in Your name.*

Store up treasure

for yourselves

in heaven.

Matthew 6:20

NOVEMBER 1st

All Saints

All Saints Day reminds us of those who lived their lives for Christ, and motivates us to follow their example.

Today is the Birthday of:

_____

_____

_____

Today is the Anniversary of:

_____

_____

Prayer: *Jesus, like the Saints in heaven may I follow wherever You lead me.*

NOVEMBER 2nd

All Souls

On All Souls Day, we pray for all those who have died and are working to attain the glories of heaven.

Today is the Birthday of:

_____

_____

_____

Today is the Anniversary of:

_____

_____

Prayer: *Father, I pray that You gather to Yourself all those I have loved and lost so that they might experience eternal peace and joy.*

NOVEMBER 3rd

St. Martin de Porres

Saint Martin, Patron of Race Relations, reminds us of God's universal love and His desire that we love one another equally.

Today is the Birthday of:

Today is the Anniversary of:

Prayer: *Loving God, help me to speak out against bigotry of any kind.*

NOVENA 4th

St. Charles Borromeo

Saint Charles Borromeo, Patron of Seminarians, teaches us to encourage those who answer God's call to religious life.

❦   ❦   ❦

Today is the Birthday of:

_____

_____

_____

Today is the Anniversary of:

_____

_____

Prayer: *Father, I thank You for the priests and seminarians You have chosen to serve Your church.*

NOVERBER 5th

St. Bertille

Saint Bertille's hospitality attracted both beggars and princesses, reminding us that Christ welcomed all who came to Him.

Today is the Birthday of:

Today is the Anniversary of:

Prayer: *Loving Jesus, help me to heed Your instruction to assist those who are less fortunate.*

NOVEMBER 6th

St. Leonard of Noblac

Patron of Prisoners, Saint Leonard shows that Jesus died and rose so that we could all be freed from the prison of sin.

Today is the Birthday of:

_____

_____

_____

Today is the Anniversary of:

_____

_____

Prayer: *Beloved Christ, let me feel in my very soul the freedom You gained for me at such a great cost.*

NOVEMBER 7th

St. Englebert, Martyr

We admire the morality of Saint Englebert, who died in his effort to prevent corruption and thievery in the Church.

Today is the Birthday of:

Today is the Anniversary of:

Prayer: *Just God, help me to be honest and give me the courage to speak out for what is right.*

NOVERMBER 8th

St. Willehad

Saint Willehad illustrates that early failure at our chosen ministries may lead to later success if we remain committed.

Today is the Birthday of:

Today is the Anniversary of:

Prayer: *Father, even when I think I have failed You, let me take heart in Your forgiving love.*

NOVEMBER 9th

Bl. Elizabeth of the Trinity

Blessed Elizabeth demonstrates great faith in her dying words, "I'm going to the light, to love, to life."

Today is the Birthday of:

Today is the Anniversary of:

Prayer: *Lord, comfort me with the knowledge that You are waiting for us all and at death will reunite me with those I love.*

NOVEMBER 10th

St. Andrew of Avellino

Like November's flower, the chrysanthemum, Saint Andrew embodies compassion in his gentle, pastoral ministering.

Today is the Birthday of:

Today is the Anniversary of:

Prayer: *Holy Spirit, embolden me to demonstrate understanding and compassion for those in need.*

NOVEMBER 11th

St. Bartholomew of Rossano

Saint Bartholomew shows us the value of completing the works of God others have started in our Christian community.

Today is the Birthday of:

Today is the Anniversary of:

Prayer: *Almighty God, show me how to continue the work of others so that Your plan may be fulfilled.*

NOVEMBER 12th

St. Josaphat, Martyr

Saint Josaphat illustrates the importance of unity in Christianity and teaches us to overcome the divisions we face.

Today is the Birthday of:

Today is the Anniversary of:

Prayer: *Creator God, help me to be actively involved in unifying the community of Christian believers.*

NOVEMBER 13th

St. Frances Xavier Cabrini

Patroness of Immigrants, Saint Frances reminds us of the Bible's direction to love and welcome strangers.

Today is the Birthday of:

Today is the Anniversary of:

Prayer: *Lord, may I be willing to share the advantages of this country with all who seek a place here.*

NOVEMBER 14th

St. Lawrence O'Toole

In seeking peace during times of upheaval, Saint Lawrence earned Jesus' blessing: "Blessed are the peacemakers."

Today is the Birthday of:

Today is the Anniversary of:

Prayer: *Jesus, help me to put aside my own combativeness to bring about peace in the world.*

NOVEMBER 15th

St. Albert the Great

Patron of Scientists, Saint Albert showed us that deep spirituality and human reason should compliment each other.

Today is the Birthday of:

Today is the Anniversary of:

Prayer: *God of all creation, through my soul and mind may I better love You and the wonders of Your world.*

NOVERMBER 16th

St. Margaret of Scotland

Saint Margaret, Patroness of Widows, illustrates that God is with us as we experience painful losses and difficult challenges.

Today is the Birthday of:

Today is the Anniversary of:

Prayer: *Father, help me to turn to You for help when my burden seems too heavy.*

NOVEMBER 17th

St. Hilda

We admire Saint Hilda's wisdom in spiritually counseling and encouraging the men and women in her monastery.

Today is the Birthday of:

Today is the Anniversary of:

Prayer: *Lord, please send me wise and comforting counselors who will bring me clarity, peace, and renewal.*

NOVERBER 18th

St. Odo of Cluny

Saint Odo demonstrates that compromise and negotiation are tools God offers to ensure peace among the nations.

Today is the Birthday of:

Today is the Anniversary of:

Prayer: *Father, let me never be so full of myself that I fail to consider the thoughts and opinions of others.*

NOVERMBER 19th

St. Mechtilde

Saint Mechtilde teaches us that because children often imitate our actions, we must be good models of Christianity.

Today is the Birthday of:

Today is the Anniversary of:

Prayer: *Jesus, help me to always lead the children in my life to You through my actions and my speech.*

NOVEMBER 20th

St. Bernward

Saint Bernward is a reminder that in disputes, we must act with restraint and treat our opponents with respect.

Today is the Birthday of:

Today is the Anniversary of:

Prayer: *Gentle God, in pursuing a resolution, help me to put aside my pride and act with Christian wisdom.*

NOVERMBER 21st

St. Gelasius I

Saint Gelasius reminds us to receive and honor Jesus' Body and Blood through the Eucharist.

Today is the Birthday of:

Today is the Anniversary of:

Prayer: *Jesus, may I ever be grateful and in awe of the privilege of receiving You in the Holy Eucharist.*

NOVERMBER 22nd

St. Cecilia, Martyr

As the Patroness of Poets and Musicians, Saint Cecilia teaches us to use our gifts to give praise and glory to God.

Today is the Birthday of:

_____

_____

_____

Today is the Anniversary of:

_____

_____

Prayer: *Father, help me to refresh my faith and my spirit through sacred poetry and music.*

NOVEMBER 23rd

St. Columban

Saint Columban illustrates the importance of creating holy places to worship God and encourage each other.

Today is the Birthday of:

Today is the Anniversary of:

Prayer: *Living God, I thank You for houses of worship where we gather to contemplate Your majesty.*

NOVEMBER 24th

St. Colman of Coyne

Saint Colman demonstrates how we can change our lives to follow God at any age and from any state of being.

Today is the Birthday of:

Today is the Anniversary of:

Prayer: *Lord, remind me that I am never too old or too enmeshed in a way of life to change everything for You.*

NOVEMBER 25th

St. Catherine of Alexandria, Martyr

Patroness of Philosophers, St. Catherine's life of great faith and courage reminds us that many great minds are fixed upon God.

Today is the Birthday of:

_____

_____

_____

Today is the Anniversary of:

_____

_____

Prayer: *Omniscient God, let me stay always mindful of You so that You may direct my intelligence.*

NOVERBER 26th

St. Leonard of Port Maurice

Patron of Parish Missions, St. Leonard emphasizes for us the beauty and importance of making the Stations of the Cross.

Today is the Birthday of:

Today is the Anniversary of:

Prayer: *Suffering Jesus, by making the Stations of the Cross, renew my appreciation for Your sacrifice.*

NOVEMBER 27th

St. Maximus

Saint Maximus exemplifies for us obedience in the way he accepted responsibilities he did not always want.

Today is the Birthday of:

Today is the Anniversary of:

Prayer: *Father, give me the strength to accept the roles You've given me and to do my best.*

NOVEMBER 28th

St. Stephen the Younger, Martyr

Saint Stephen underwent many agonies in his support of sacred images, revealing their value as aids to worship.

Today is the Birthday of:

Today is the Anniversary of:

Prayer: *Lord, I thank You for inspiring artists to create the holy images that encourage all Christians.*

NOVERMBER 29th

St. Saturninus, Martyr

Saint Saturninus shows us how idolatry can be eliminated by God's gifts of inspired preaching and miracles.

Today is the Birthday of:

Today is the Anniversary of:

Prayer: *Watchful God, move me to successfully and vigorously oppose idolatry in its many forms.*

NOVEMBER 30th

St. Andrew, Apostle

Brother of the Apostle and first pope, Peter, Saint Andrew demonstrates the importance of collaboration in fostering faith.

Today is the Birthday of:

_____

_____

_____

Today is the Anniversary of:

_____

_____

Prayer: *Jesus, I thank You for drawing men and women to You who created a strong foundation for Your message.*

Love Jesus
and
keep Him
for thy Friend.

Bk. 2, 7.
Imitation of Christ

DECENBER 1st

St. Florence

Convert and laywoman, Florence exemplifies single-minded devotion to God and His Kingdom.

Today is the Birthday of:

Today is the Anniversary of:

Prayer: *Father, help me to never hesitate in turning my choice of work or lifestyle into Your choice.*

DECEMBER 2nd

St. Habakkuk, Prophet

A Hebrew prophet who emphasized God's ties to His people, Habakkuk illustrates that God always welcomes us back.

Today is the Birthday of:

Today is the Anniversary of:

Prayer: *Lord, if I stray from You, remind me that You wait for me to return to Your embrace.*

DECEMBER 3rd

St. Francis Xavier

Patron of Foreign Missions, Saint Francis reminds us that we must always be willing to stretch our limits when working for God.

Today is the Birthday of:

Today is the Anniversary of:

Prayer: *God of all, bring me to the place where I can do the most good.*

DECEMBER 4th

St. Barbara

Saint Barbara, Patroness of Builders, shows us how buildings can give glory to God.

Today is the Birthday of:

Today is the Anniversary of:

Prayer: *Lord, build Your house in my heart and soul so that others may see You in me.*

DECEMBER 5th

St. Gerald

Saint Gerald reminds us to never cease to review and reform our spiritual selves.

Today is the Birthday of:

Today is the Anniversary of:

Prayer: *Father, help me to be constantly on guard against slipping into selfishness or sin.*

DECEMBER 6th

St. Nicholas

Patron of Children, Saint Nicholas symbolizes the need to celebrate God's gift of Jesus to us by giving to others.

Today is the Birthday of:

Today is the Anniversary of:

Prayer: *Generous Lord, help me to celebrate the joy of Your birth with the happy abandon of a child.*

DECEMBER 7th

St. Ambrose

Patron of Candlemakers, Saint Ambrose reminds us that we must not keep the light of the Lord hidden within us.

Today is the Birthday of:

Today is the Anniversary of:

Prayer: *Jesus, remind me to let the light You've sparked within me shine out joyously.*

DECEMBER 8th

*Immaculate Conception
of the Blessed Virgin Mary*

Patroness of the United States, the Immaculate Conception shows how completely God loved us by preparing the perfect mother for Jesus.

Today is the Birthday of:

Today is the Anniversary of:

Prayer: *Loving Father, open my eyes so that I can see the many wonders and signs You've given to us.*

DECEMBER 9th

St. Juan Diego

Saint Juan Diego illustrates how radically we may be changed by an encounter with Jesus or His Blessed Mother.

Today is the Birthday of:

Today is the Anniversary of:

Prayer: *Lord, help me to embrace the changes that result from sacred encounters.*

DECEMBER 10th

St. Gregory III

Pope Gregory's affection for the poor, widows, orphans, and the clergy teaches us what kind of leaders we should follow.

Today is the Birthday of:

Today is the Anniversary of:

Prayer: *God, I pray for strong, loving church leaders who teach Your precepts with compassion.*

DECEMBER 11th

St. Damasus I

Pope St. Damasus shows us that we all have different gifts and should use them in the way God directs us.

Today is the Birthday of:

_____

_____

_____

Today is the Anniversary of:

_____

_____

Prayer: *Lord, please guide me in the way I use my gifts and prevent me from ever using them to do harm.*

DECEMBER 12th

Our Lady of Guadalupe

The faithful of Mexico and the United States are united in their devotion to the Patroness of the Americas.

❧   ❧   ❧

Today is the Birthday of:

_____

_____

_____

Today is the Anniversary of:

_____

_____

Prayer: *God of loving kindness, thank You for the love that all people share for Your Mother Mary.*

DECEMBER 13th

St. Lucy, Martyr

Saint Lucy, Patroness of the Blind, warns us not to be blinded by the desire for worldly goods or power.

Today is the Birthday of:

Today is the Anniversary of:

Prayer: *Father, help me to see that it is You in Whom all my desires are truly met.*

DECENBER 14th

St. Venantius Fortunatus

The liturgical writing of Saint Venantius celebrates how Jesus triumphed over suffering and redeemed us on the Cross.

Today is the Birthday of:

Today is the Anniversary of:

Prayer: *Lord, I praise You in hymns like* Pange Lingua Glorioso *which raise my mind and heart to You.*

DECEMBER 15th

St. Maximin of Mesmin

Saint Maximin reminds us how Jesus fed thousands with scraps of food and inspires us to share our plenty with the hungry.

Today is the Birthday of:

Today is the Anniversary of:

Prayer: *Generous Jesus, today in Your name, I will make a donation of food or money for the hungry.*

DECEMBER 16th

St. Adelaide

Saint Adelaide, Patroness of Prisoners, demonstrates that we are all imprisoned by sin and are freed only by God.

Today is the Birthday of:

Today is the Anniversary of:

Prayer: *God of all salvation, help me to repent and avoid all sin.*

DECEMBER 17th

St. Begga

Saint Begga shows us how we can use the loss of loved ones to promote God's plan and the faith of others.

గొ‌‌‌ఇ   గొ‌‌‌ఇ   గొ‌‌‌ఇ

Today is the Birthday of:

_____

_____

_____

Today is the Anniversary of:

_____

_____

Prayer: *Father, may I never miss an opportunity to turn grief into joy for myself and others by following You.*

DECEMBER 18th

St. Gatian

Saint Gatian demonstrates that we do not need massive, ornate churches to worship God and receive the Holy Eucharist.

༺༻ ༺༻ ༺༻

Today is the Birthday of:

Today is the Anniversary of:

Prayer: *God of all creation, help me to remember that I can worship and adore You wherever I am.*

DECEMBER 19th

St. Anastasius I

Saint Anastasius, a pope who rejected the wealth of his office, reminds us that Jesus lived in poverty and humility.

Today is the Birthday of:

_____

_____

_____

Today is the Anniversary of:

_____

_____

Prayer: *Father, help me to remember that we have little need for wealth when we put You first.*

DECEMBER 20th

St. Philogonius

Like December's flower, the holly, which symbolizes success, Philogonius as bishop protected the Church during difficult times.

Today is the Birthday of:

Today is the Anniversary of:

Prayer: *Lord, please give me the strength to succeed in protecting the faith You have given me.*

DECEMBER 21st

St. Micah, Prophet

Saint Micah reminds us that as the Messiah, Jesus came to bring peace and love to all women and men.

Today is the Birthday of:

Today is the Anniversary of:

Prayer: *Jesus Messiah, fill my heart with peace and a sense of communion with all my brothers and sisters.*

DECEMBER 22nd

St. Chaeremon, Martyr

Saint Chaeremon illustrates that the Middle East has been a place where faith has always been challenged.

Today is the Birthday of:

Today is the Anniversary of:

Prayer: *Lord of All, when I feel despair about the Middle East, comfort me with Your all-embracing love.*

DECEMBER 23rd

St. John of Kanty

Saint John reminds us of the importance of abstinence and sacrifice as disciplines in our personal journeys of faith.

Today is the Birthday of:

Today is the Anniversary of:

Prayer: *Father, today I will give up something I enjoy as a sacrifice to You and a discipline to me.*

DECEMBER 24th

∽∼∾

St. Irmina

St. Irmina illustrates how good things can come from unexpected tragedies if we reject despair and put our trust in God.

༺❀༻ ༺❀༻ ༺❀༻

Today is the Birthday of:

_____

_____

_____

Today is the Anniversary of:

_____

_____

Prayer: *Father, lead me to respond in a positive Christian manner when terrible things happen to me or to others.*

DECEMBER 25th

Christmas Day

Christmas Day and every event leading to Jesus' Nativity shows that God works though all things: nature, geography, humankind.

Today is the Birthday of:

Today is the Anniversary of:

Prayer: *God of heaven and earth, on this day I rejoice in Your Son, Jesus Christ, and in all creation.*

DECEMBER 26th

St. Stephen, Martyr

Saint Stephen, the first Martyr for Jesus, demonstrates that the violence of men and women cannot undo God's love and protection.

Today is the Birthday of:

Today is the Anniversary of:

Prayer: *Father when I am fearful about the violence in the world, be my refuge and my peace.*

DECEMBER 27th

St. John, Apostle and Evangelist

Saint John, the "apostle whom Jesus loved," inspires us to imitate him in extolling and praising Jesus to everyone.

Today is the Birthday of:

Today is the Anniversary of:

Prayer: *Jesus, give me the grace, courage, and evagelizing power of John despite my unworthiness.*

DECEMBER 28th

St. Antony of Lerins

Saint Antony illustrates that it is often more helpful to others if we live our faith rather than just talk about it.

Today is the Birthday of:

Today is the Anniversary of:

Prayer: *Perfect God, lead me to act in ways today that will show my faith to everyone I meet.*

DECEMBER 29th

St. David, King and Prophet

Saint David, chosen and forgiven by God despite sinning, teaches that we must repent deeply when we wrong God and others.

❦   ❦   ❦

Today is the Birthday of:

Today is the Anniversary of:

Prayer: *Forgiving God, like David, I, too, seek Your forgiveness for my sins and the wrongs I do to others.*

DECEMBER 30th

St. Anysius

A dedicated bishop, Saint Anysius reminds us to encourage our clergy and to lead others by our own example.

Today is the Birthday of:

Today is the Anniversary of:

Prayer: *Father, help me to be a good, Christian mentor to those who turn to me for guidance.*

DECEMBER 31st

St. John Francis Regis

Saint John Francis Regis, Patron of Medical Social Workers, reminds us at the New Year of Jesus' instruction to visit the sick.

Today is the Birthday of:

_____

_____

_____

Today is the Anniversary of:

_____

_____

Prayer: *Beloved Jesus, instead of feeling sorry for myself in this coming year, let me visit someone who is ill.*